Kelly and Tosha are cut from the same cloth as Dan Cathy, Chick-fil-A. What does the comparison have to do with the book you're about to read? Well, I have known Kelly and Tosha for many years now and I can tell you they are not afraid to dive into those potentially awkward situations with "sinners." In fact, they've been forging those unlikely relationships right here in Colorado Springs, which is not necessarily as "conservative" or "Christian" a community as you might think.

Kelly is not a compromiser when it comes to his faith in Jesus but, as he puts it, we need to be ready to "take risks to reach the lost." That's what this book is about.

Jim Daly,
President
Focus On The Family

Compassion International is honored to partner with pastors like Kelly Williams who are committed to leading Jesus followers to become more like Him, a Friend of Sinners, taking risks to reach the lost. I invite you to join Kelly on this risk-taking journey through the pages of this book.

Santiago "Jimmy" Mellado
President and CEO, Compassion International

Kelly Williams and the church he pastors don't play it safe. They've taken lots of risks to reach people who are far from God. Sometimes the risks pan out. Sometimes they don't. That's not the point. The point is their willingness to do whatever it takes to reach out to bring back to Jesus the people he died for. If you're tired of playing it safe, this is the book for you.

Larry Osborne
Pastor and Author, North Coast Church
Southern California

Sharing the Gospel can be as easy as making friends, but you have to take risks. Learn the real-life lessons, heartaches, and triumphs as one church became the Friend of Sinners. You'll be in good company!

David Chrzan
Pastor, Chief of Staff and Global Initiatives
Saddleback Church
Southern California

Kelly and Tosha Williams have inspired me and thousands of others through their ministry and friendship. They don't just talk about being in relationship with those who don't follow Christ. They model relationship beautifully, allowing God to use them in unexpected, eternity-changing ways, and then they share how to step into the heart of Christ's ministry by befriending those who don't know Him. Friend of Sinners *is so much more than a book. It's the story of a journey that changed my perspective and ultimately my life. I hope it will change yours as well.*

Melanie Dobson
Award-winning author of "Chateau of Secrets" and
"The Silent Order"
Founding Member of Vanguard Church
Portland, Oregon

I love Kelly Williams' Friend of Sinners *for several reasons. It is an engaging and personal account of the ups and downs of starting a church. It's a realistic description of the challenges of focusing on reaching people far from God. Vanguard Church is not only a successful church plant, it is a multiplying church that is intentionally starting new congregations. And lastly, Kelly serves the city that I also love and served as a pastor. I welcomed him when he came to town in 1997 and our city is a better place today because of Vanguard Church. This book is full of helpful tools and insights on how to start and be a church for the unchurched regardless of what city you live in. Many church planters come to Colorado Springs, few succeed. Kelly succeeded. This is his story. I loved it. You will love it too!*

Jim Tomberlin, Founder and CEO of MultiSite Solutions and
Author of *125 Tips for MultiSite Churches, Better Together:
Making Church Mergers Work,* and *Church Locality*

*I am so thankful for Pastor Kelly's unrelenting commitment to reach
everyone in our city with the Good News. This book will encourage
and strengthen you to be a faithful witness of Christ in a world that
desperately needs hope and healing.*

Brady Boyd
Senior Pastor
New Life Church, Colorado Springs, CO
Author of *"Speak Life."*

*For as long as I've known him, Pastor Kelly Williams has a had a deep
passion for people to know Jesus. These stories will spark the same
passion in you. They will inspire you to believe that God can use you
to show the love of Jesus to those right around you. I am grateful for
Vanguard Church's witness in our city, and for the way they have taken
risks to welcome people into the family of God.*

Glenn Packiam
Pastor, New Life Downtown
Colorado Springs, CO

In the book Friend of Sinners, *Pastor Kelly Williams describes how
he has led Vanguard Church to do just that. It has been my privilege
to observe first hand for twenty years how Kelly has led his church to
engage the lost community and fleshed out the example Jesus gave us to
take risks to reach the lost. I have personally known Kelly and partnered
with a number of events Kelly describes in this book and can vouch for
the effectiveness of them. As a longtime pastor, resident, and Church
Planting Catalyst in Colorado Springs, I have seen the positive impact
Vanguard Church has had in our city.*

Bill Lighty
Area Missionary/Church Planting Catalyst of the
Pikes Peak Baptist Association

In these pages, you will read Kelly's passion in obedience to our Lord to indeed be a Friend of Sinners.

Jon Elsberry
Retired Wesleyan Pastor and Kelly's longtime prayer intercessor

I have known Kelly Williams for many years. We've had our ups and downs and the mutual respect we have for each other has always made the problems solvable. We do come from different backgrounds, Christian and Jewish, but respect and good communication has never let religion become an issue. Kelly and myself are problem solvers and the mutual respect with honest and open communication has always proved to be the answer every time. As a matter of fact most all of our agreements were finalized by a handshake before being written up into print. That's what mutual respect brings to the table.

Larry Melnick
Business Owner
Colorado Springs, CO

I've known Kelly for over twenty years. His heart for the lost is the real deal, and his steps to reach people are practical and proven. The thousands of people who have come to Christ through Kelly's leadership reminds me the risks are worth it!

Thomas Thompson
Senior Pastor
Pulpit Rock Church, Colorado Springs

Kelly combines vision, passionate risk-taking, and a steady hand born of experience to lead a vibrant community of believers in our rapidly-shifting culture. As the founding pastor of Vanguard Church, he has faithfully shaped an innovative church culture. The scope and impact of Vanguard is international, and for me ... personal. As you read Friend of Sinners, *Williams will move you both to reach and risk more for the sake of Christ's Kingdom.*

Armin Sommer
Senior Pastor
Grace Church on The Mount
Netcong, New Jersey

Every faith leader I encounter is looking for stories of real people being transformed by the Gospel and principles for how we apply this to our life and ministry. You will find real stories and usable principles packed into the pages of Friend of Sinners. *I have had the privilege of sitting under Kelly's leadership for the last ten years, and the best part about this book is he lives out every word. Read* Friend of Sinners *and you will be re-invited into God's relentless pursuit of people!*

Alan Briggs, Multiply Pastor Vanguard Church,
Director of Frontline Church Planting,
Author of *Staying is the new Going, Guardrails*
Colorado Springs, Colorado

In 2006 on a visit to Colorado Springs, Pastor Kelly and I were introduced at Vanguard Church and remain friends to this day. His story is candid and honest with the power to inspire. The questions posed at the end of every chapter encourages self-reflection with the knowledge that the Holy Spirit will guide and transform as we forge ahead in our own stories. He's enthusiastic and gutsy in his approach to life. Friend of Sinners *is a must-read.*

Craig Whittaker
Lead Pastor of Capo Beach Church in Southern California
Dana Point, CA

One of my first encounters with Kelly was at a Community Discussion regarding LGBT held at the church he leads. That forum was bold, risky, and it was fruitful. He's become a great friend and from time to time he lets me in on the newest opportunity he's pursuing. It's inspiring to me that Kelly is drawn to the edges, reaching out to and taking risks for the overlooked.

John Pauls
Senior Pastor
Austin Bluffs Community Church
Colorado Springs, Colorado

Kelly Williams is tenacious in his desire to build bridges with those who feel like outcasts to the Good News of Christ. Inviting and loving ALL people into a real relationship with Jesus Christ is Kelly's passion. Having known Kelly for over fifteen years, I bear witness that he is the real deal and can be trusted, and his loving and relational approach to reaching the lost should be studied by anyone who desires to do the same.

Vance Brown
Founder, Band of Brothers Ministry
Author, *No Matter the Cost*
Colorado Springs, CO

I have known Kelly for three decades since we were randomly placed together as roommates our freshman year at Liberty University. Throughout these years, Kelly has consistently demonstrated the courage to take great risk in loving people into a real relationship with Jesus Christ. Some of these risks, like starting Vanguard Church were public, but most are hidden within his lifestyle of quietly engaging people in a Christ-shaped, self-giving love. I can think of no one better teacher to both remind us and to guide us into a life of courageous risk in following after the Friend of Sinners.

Joel Willitts, PhD
Professor of Biblical and Theological Studies North Park University
Chicago, IL

I'm truly lucky to have Pastor Williams as my personal friend and a great partner in building community across the ideological spectrum. After our ferocious debates, we often come to a meeting of the minds. And when we don't, at least I know I've debated and disagreed with a smart, caring, and IMHO slightly misguided man. This book will help you understand what makes Kelly tick.

John Weiss
Founder of The Colorado Springs Independent Newspaper
The Pikes Peak Region's largest locally owned newspaper
with 125,000 loyal readers

To my dad, Larry Williams.

Thanks for dreaming, Dad!

Your dream not only became my dream, but now also God's will for my life.

CONTENTS

Foreword

A few years ago, there was a lot of news circulating over the fact that Chick-fil-A—a business well-known for being rooted in Christian values—was donating money to organizations that had been deemed "anti-gay." Not surprisingly, this resulted in protests and boycotts against the restaurant chain on the part of some pro-LGBT groups. One group in particular, Campus Pride, orchestrated a national campaign against Chick-fil-A and other businesses that supported traditional marriage.

But then something unexpected happened. Dan Cathy, the COO of Chick-fil-A (and a personal friend of mine), took a risk and *reached out*. Specifically, he called Shane Windmeyer, the executive director of Campus Pride. In an article for the *Huffington Post*, Mr. Windmeyer wrote: "I took the call with great caution. He was going to tear me apart, right? Give me a piece of his mind? Turn his lawyers on me?" But in fact, there was no "agenda" behind Dan's phone call other than to listen and to talk. Over the following weeks and months, Dan and Shane would meet on several occasions to dialogue on the issues, but also to just get to know one another better.

"Through all this," Mr. Windmeyer writes, "Dan and I shared respectful, enduring communication and built trust. His demeanor has always been one of kindness and openness. Even when I continued to directly question his public actions and the funding decisions, Dan embraced the opportunity to have dialogue and hear my perspective."

Eventually, Mr. Windmeyer ended up attending the 2012 Chick-fil-A Bowl game between LSU and Clemson—as a personal guest of Dan Cathy and his family. Mr. Windmeyer's accounting of the event in the *Huffington Post* went viral and became a national news story. Dan Cathy's willingness to reach across the aisle and be a friend of "sinners" had caused the world to sit up and take notice.

Throughout this remarkable series of events, Dan Cathy did not compromise his beliefs on the authority of Scripture or the sanctity of biblical marriage. And Shane Windmeyer did not abandon his pursuit of furthering a pro-LGBT agenda. Nevertheless, Dan's willingness to reach out and foster a *friendship* with Shane enabled them to see one another as real people rather than as faceless opponents or pawns in the battle of worldviews.

Here's how Mr. Windmeyer summed up the experience:

"Throughout the conversations Dan expressed a sincere interest in my life, wanting to get to know me on a personal level. He wanted to know about where I grew up, my faith, my family, even my husband, Tommy. In return, I learned about his wife and kids and gained an appreciation for his devout belief in Jesus Christ and his commitment to being 'a follower of Christ' more than a 'Christian.'"[1]

Who can say what seeds were planted as a result of Dan's willingness to befriend Shane? We may never know. But as our culture becomes more and more polarized, we should ask ourselves how we can be used by the Lord to help turn hearts toward Him if we're not willing to sit and listen to the hearts of those who don't acknowledge Him as Lord. We don't have to compromise our principles in order to forge fellowship with those who don't embrace those same principles. If we're willing to reach out with Christlike love, the opportunities are limitless. As Solomon reminds us, "When a man's ways please the Lord, He makes even his enemies live at peace with him" (Proverbs 16:7 ESV).

What does all of this have to do with the book you're about to read? Well, I have known Kelly and Tosha Williams for many years now, and I can tell you that they are cut from the same cloth as Dan Cathy. They're not afraid to dive into those potentially awkward situations with "sinners." In fact, they've been forging those unlikely relationships right here in Colorado Springs, which is not necessarily as "conservative" or "Christian" a community as you might think.

But for the sake of the Kingdom—for the sake of Christ and making Him known—they are willing to engage with a broad range of unlikely characters. And for that reason, you will read about some genuinely awkward encounters in the pages that follow. You'll also sense Kelly's trademark passion and intensity in these pages. For those reasons and more, some of this may make you feel uncomfortable. Some of it you might not even fully agree with. In fact, in a few places I might have even taken a different approach.

But make no mistake—Kelly is not a compromiser when it comes to his faith. He wants to see people encounter Christ and welcome them into a vibrant, diverse community of faith. He's so committed to that, in fact, that he's willing to think outside the box—sometimes *way* outside the box—to make it happen!

The apostle Paul reminds us that "God showed his great love for us by sending Christ to die for us while we were still sinners" (Romans 5:8 TLB). "While we were still sinners...." God didn't wait for us to clean up our act before He sent His Son to engage and interact with us. Nor should we avoid investing in and building genuine relationships with those who look, believe, and behave differently than us.

We just need to be willing to step outside of our comfort zones. Or, as Kelly puts it, we need to be ready to "take risks to reach the lost." That's what this book is about.

Jim Daly
President, Focus on the Family

Acknowledgment

My dad, Larry Williams, dreamed of starting a church in Kentucky called "Victory Baptist Church." He never did it. Sometimes people ask me, "Where did your desire to start a church first come from?" Looking back, I now know. God used my dad's dream to birth His dream in me. Just like King David, he didn't build the Temple, but his son, Solomon, did. Vanguard was birthed in the mind of God, but was sent to earth through my earthly father to me. When I went off to college in 1989, the dream was already inside of me thanks to my dad. Thanks also to Phillip Coomer who introduced me to Dr. Norm Geisler. His book *The Infiltration of the New Age Movement* jazzed me to start a church in a state I had never visited. And as they say, "the rest is history!"

Over the years I have MANY people to thank for their investment in Vanguard, not least of which the Southern Baptist Convention for believing in us and helping us start Vanguard. I am forever grateful. I also want to thank the following people who made Vanguard a reality in one way or another:

My childhood:

Larry and Linda Sue Williams, Coral Hill Baptist Church, Ray and Linda Woodie, Richard Thomas, Phillip and Sharon Coomer, Steve and Debbie Williams, Harry and Marilyn Williams, Martha Jo Hurt

My college years:

Liberty University, Dr. Jerry Falwell, Dr. Norm Giesler, Dr. Joel R. Willitts, Tosha Lamdin Williams, Larry and Margaret Williams, Darren Child, Dr. Paul Fink, George Cannon

My seminary years:

Dallas Theological Seminary, Dr. Timothy Warren, Dr. Bill Lawerence, Dr. John Hannah, Dr. Chuck Swindoll, Dr. Rick Warren, Dr. Bob Reccord, Dr. John and Sharon Yeats, South Park Baptist Church

My church years:

Pikes Peak Baptist Association, Colorado Baptist, Chapel Hills Baptist Church, Crossroads Church, Bill and Carol Lighty, Greg and Cheryl Cole, Charlie and Evelyn Aiken, Dr. Vern Henderson, Bill Dodson, Ray and Ann Pokorny, Brian and Kirstan Beatty, Jon and Melanie Dobson, Jen McLendon, Steve and Jan Leitz, Dr. Kutter and Jessica Callaway, Nathan Fischer, Mike and Yvette Mihaly, Tim and Amy Arseneau, Rick and Laura Clapp, Donavan and Holly Kerr, Rick and Laura Wesselhoff, Bart and Sallie Mann, Chris and Sandy Benson, Jeff and Mindy Kiepke, Chris and Shannon Misner, Steve and Ellen Goad, David and Mandy Houle, Jon and Sandi Elsberry, Richie and Dana Fike, Alan and Julie Briggs, Josh Burcham, Larry Melnick, John Weiss, Vance and Betsy Brown, John and Sue Cressman, Big John and Phoebe Cressman.

Seth and Laurie Grotelueschen, Chris and Laura Fowler, Community Church Builder, Larry Osborne, Jim Tomberline, Jim Daly, Dr. James Dobson, David Chrzan, Craig and Jeannie Whitaker, Mike and Kris Helwege, Marty and Cindy Rauer, Ray and Debra Woolridge, Dion and Andrea Heisler, Bob and Laura Schwarz, Craig and Candice Covak, Brian and Debbie Cichowitz, Paul and Deanne Yankey, Tony and Becky Metcalf, David and Renee Hames, Joel and Holly Malick, David and Jessica Bair, Steve and Michelle Zitzmann, Andrea Smith, Mike and Tabitha Clinton, John and Cristine Wilson, Seth and Angela Swartz, Jerry Tolley, Deb Guida, William Beeler, Allen Robinson, Gary and Virginia Johnston, Eileen Larkin, and Scott and Heidi White.

Torie Harvey, Matt and Tricia Vincent, Joe and Carrie Gilbert, Jim and Jessie Whitlock, Bill and Melanie Waugaman, Rand and Esther Clark, Chuck and Mary McKenzie, Josh and Wendy Neal, Andrew and Angelica Mersereau, Chris and Holly Port, Lori Sanders, Sarah Jackson, Matt and Stacy Ricci, Sam Taylor, John and Gay Williams, Andrew and Jana Hanna, John and Linda Sorensen, Luke and Trisha Barfield, Josh and Alli Hunter, Chad and Leesha Mecham, Nate and Renee Stewart, Rick and Kim McKenna, Chad and Kara Livingston, Tamara Parks, Steve and Cindi Bruger, Debbie Navarre, Stuart and Jana Lundh, Chris and Stephanie Haggerty, Ryan and Wendy Cross, Scott Cline, Bria Cline, Jeff and Laura Sharda, Heather Gardner, Tom and Danae Herndon, Trevor and Jill Eich, Rob and Karen Veghte, Jan Jones, Kim Lowe, Jim and Joanne Lowe, and Jim Martin.

Tad and Laura Lazechko, Matt Mead, Catrina Massey, Mike and Jill McCoy, Jonathan and Ashley Madrid, Andrew Perkett (A.K.A. Carl), Kimberly Woolridge, Joshua and Rachelle Stephenson, Justin and Rachel Wickline, Guillermo and Amber Guevara, Nathan and Melissa Paisley, Crystalyn Johnson, Kimberly Barry,

Holly Berthiaume, Clinton and Erica Cooper, Robyn Clark, Dexter Dennis, Mike and Teri Diamond, Jared and Emma Grace Goad, Lucas Goad, Noah Goad, Amiah Goad, Maea and Leah Apineru, Kirk and Erica Bode, Micah and Becca Haarbrink, Ryan and Danae Gillespie, Paul Martinez, Evan (Almighty) Hopper, Mark and Stephanie Krug, Nancy McGray, Darrin and Brenna Gregg, Jeremy and Amanda Gibson, Austin and Monica Glenn, Matt and Shaina Glenn, Marc and Karen Plaskie, Rosie Siver, Mike Smith, Marty and Martha Taylor, Jeff and August Jimeson, Laurie Kohere, Matt and Anna McCabe, Patty Adair, Joe Herman, and Rick Morley

Stewart McKee, Kevin and Melissa Feldotto, Nate Schwarz, Caleb Schwarz, Caleb Miller, Micah Schwarz, Maddie Schwarz, Rob Smit, Vic Dallin, Alisha Mann, Mark and Patty Morrissey, David Lalonde, Charlie Gilbert, Christian Gilbert, Harlan and Kaye Seeliger, Velma Knierem, Elaine Elsberry, Dave May, The Vanguard Worship Team, Steve and Jamie Neal, Rod and Cari Pemberton, George and Sue Mulhern, Paula Stern, Marv and Ann Wooten, Sam Wooten, John Eldredge, Melissa Pritchard, Joe Damewood, Wes and Beth Schlauch, The Lowe Family, The Eich Family, The Briggs Family, Steve and Suzanne Sharpe, Dave and Emma Johnson, Kathleen Woolridge, Jonathan and Roxanne Woolridge, Phillip Woolridge, Grace Covak, Elijah Covak, Judson Covak, Doug and Priscilla Sparks, Steve and Tara Caton, Gary and Kim Trobee, Sean and Kathy Buchanan, Jacob Pace, Jordan Pace, Ron and Mel Miller, Brent and Cathy Holmcombe, Chiceaux and Joy Lynch, Bill and Kathleen Nehring, John and Jenny Marshall, Steve & Emily Moeller, Claudia Martinez, Ken and Jessica Medley, and Shari Edgell Walker.

It was difficult to decide who to put on this list because I could have written a whole book of names in gratitude for countless others. I chose the names I did because they represent moments in time that were critical to Vanguard coming into existence, and also some demonstrate long-term service to Vanguard, especially during critical moments that kept it alive and thriving for these past twenty years through faithful stewardship.

I want to thank, in closing, countless Vanguard staff, deacons, directors, elders, and prayer warriors, along with countless other Vanguard members and volunteers. Because of your faithfulness, we have seen 3188 people so far give their lives to Jesus and be baptized through Vanguard. Heaven is bigger because of you! We have also partnered to plant forty-two churches so far. We have a long way to go to reaching 50k souls with the Gospel and planting 5k churches; the names on this list are sure to grow as we continue to take risks to be a Friend of Sinners as we love more people into a real relationship with Jesus Christ and multiply disciples, leaders, and churches for the Glory of Jesus. Thank you to all who have made this dream a reality!

In closing, I want to especially thank Crosslink for publishing this book. And last but not least, thank you to my Beloved Tosha and my five amazing children: Anastasha, Christianna, Joshua, Annalarie, and Journey Grace. Thanks for making this journey meaningful in ways only family can. Love you muches!

Introduction

"Colorado Springs is the last place in the world I would start a church."

Pastor Rick Warren's words to me at the June 1996 Southern Baptist Convention in New Orleans took me a bit aback.

We had just graduated from seminary and were serving as interim pastors at South Park Baptist Church in Grand Prairie, Texas. The church sent Tosha and me to the convention to represent them. This was an unexpected privilege for a couple of young twenty-ish adults. We felt quite splurged having an all-expense paid trip to New Orleans and marveled at our fortune as we walked the French Quarter after sessions.

We must admit: we had ulterior motives for going. We had long felt God's calling for us to be church planters. We went to the convention trying to discern where God wanted us to plant a church and with whom. Would we "stay" Southern Baptist?

After a session at the convention, we visited with Pastor Warren, a Southern Baptist in Southern California, to have him sign our copy of his book.

Heart beating fast, we walked up to his book signing table and handed Pastor Warren his book, *Purpose Driven Church*.

We said, "Pastor Rick, can we ask you a question?"

He responded, "Yes," with a smile.

"If you were starting a church today, where would you start it?"

He paused then responded, "Las Vegas."

Pastor Rick must have seen the puzzled look on my face, so he asked me a question. "Where are you thinking of starting one?"

We said, "Colorado Springs."

He said with a forced smile, "That is the last place in the world I would start a church."

Right then, we thought, *Then it must be the place.*

We don't tell you this story to throw Pastor Rick Warren under the proverbial bus. We don't tell this story because it was our catalyst to prove wrong the church-planting guru of the west. We have nothing but the greatest of admiration and appreciation for Pastor Rick Warren. Matter a fact, many years later, his chief of staff at Saddleback Church, David Chrzan, has become a dear friend of ours and has spoken at our annual Multiply Conference at Vanguard in Colorado Springs.

We tell you this story because we have since learned that *God's will for you may not make sense to other very godly people that you look up to in your life.*

God has each of us on a journey. We agree with Pastor Rick that the last place in the world we would "want" to start a church is in the "Christian mecca" of the world. But what many did not realize back in the nineties was that Colorado Springs had many Christian organizations but not so many Christians.

Over 80 percent of the Springs population does not attend church. Since the nineties, the Springs' church attendance has fallen below the national average. Just recently, we saw a statistic that says 82 percent of our Christian mecca goes to church *nowhere*. We are just behind Vermont in statewide church attendance.

Wow!

Welcome to postmodernity, post-God, post-Church, post-Christian America. If the "Christian mecca" is this unchristian, then we believe it is safe to say that our entire country is not as Christian as we would like to think.

So, what do we do? Do we retreat? Do we live as if the Great Commission is not in the Bible?

Jesus said to His first disciples, "I will build my church and the gates of hell will not prevail against it." We used to think of the gates of hell like bars on the doors of the church, but then we began to understand that the bars are on the gates of hell and the church is suppose to take the keys that Jesus has given us and unlock the doors of death, hell, and the grave and go into the hell of this world and fight to rescue people.

It is time to quit cursing the darkness of this world and start seeking ways to multiply Jesus by becoming a "friend of sinners" like Jesus, but to do this, we have to give up our preconceived Christian religious views of this world.

Jesus is not shaken by the changes of this world; He is not miffed by the fact that even the Christian meccas are not so Christian anymore. His church is still going forward; His kingdom is still advancing; His will *will* be accomplished.

The question is: will we be a part of His vanguard who helps make this happen?

Will we learn how to be a "friend of sinners," or will we give up? Will we share the Gospel, or will we become modern judgmental Pharisees? Will we strategically evangelize, or will we shrug and say "what's the point"?

The point is that the world is waiting for us to love it. The world is waiting for us to unlock the doors of the hell they live in, go in, and become a friend to them like Jesus.

Are you afraid?

Good. So are we.

And by the way, so are they. We all have something in common.

Remember this: God can take us from "religion" to "friendship with sinners." This can change our lives and others' forever for eternity.

It's worth the risks!

Will you join us in this journey of taking risks to reach the lost?

CHAPTER 1

Come to Colorado Springs

"You should come to Colorado Springs."

It is the spring of 1996 and Tosha and I are called and prepared to plant a church—we just don't know where. How in the world does a church planter narrow down God's calling to one particular place?

As we try to figure out the *where*, we talk to an old college friend who lives in Colorado Springs. Melanie Beroth (Dobson now) works for Focus on the Family, is single and churchless.

When Melanie visited us in Dallas, she told us that we should really consider starting a church in Colorado Springs. We listened but, honestly, we were not interested. We had briefly visited the Springs before, stopped for a tour of Focus and for a drink of water in Manitou. Seemed like a nice place to visit, even a nice place to live—but to start a church? Not so much!

The last place in the world we wanted to go to was "Christian Mecca." We wanted our work to be strategic, meaningful, not just another option for church-hopping believers. Still, as we listened to Melanie tell us about all the young singles in Colorado Springs and about the lack of what was coined "Gen X" ministry, we considered her request.

Why not at least visit? we decided. So, several months later, on a scorching July afternoon in Dallas, we boarded a plane and stepped off into the tranquil and slightly chilly evening in Colorado Springs. We were there for a week to visit all the Front Range of Colorado. We really didn't think we will end up starting a church in Colorado Springs; we were leaning more toward Denver, Ft. Collins, or several other cities across the United States.

We just could not envision ourselves doing ministry in Colorado Springs, but we liked Melanie a lot. That is, we could not see it until we got here and began to meet people. Melanie arranged for us to meet some of her friends and we began to share our hearts and dreams of reaching people with the love of Jesus Christ.

As the week wore on, God broke our hearts for the city. He gave us a passion and a sense of calling for the people of the Springs. *Reaching people requires a heart that is broken for the people that it is seeking to reach.*

Walking down the streets of Colorado Springs, we felt our hearts breaking for total strangers. We sensed the brokenness of their lives as well as the love that Christ wanted us to have for them.

The last night we were here, I walked out on to the deck of Melanie's apartment and prayed. "Lord, do you want us here?" Immediately, I began crying uncontrollably. What is this? What is happening to me? Why am I such an emotional mess? I can neither explain nor make sense of this experience. We just know we have found the place where God wanted us to bring the love of Jesus and begin to learn how to be "a friend of sinners" like Jesus.

During our visit, we met with the local Southern Baptist associational missionary, Charlie Aiken. He warned us that

Colorado was a graveyard for church planters. Ouch! That was unexpected! Nonetheless, with youthful zeal, we charged ahead, sharing with him our ideas of how to reach this city with the love of Jesus Christ.

Charlie was a bit weirded-out by some of our ideas, but he was willing to do whatever it took to reach our city with the Gospel. He thought for a minute and said, "We had bingo in my generation, so let's try your approach."

After having met with various church leaders across the country who told us everything we could *not* do in church planting, Charlie was a breath of fresh air. We laughed out loud at his words, but we drank in his belief in two crazy young church planters. A lifetime ministry friendship was forged.

So, we headed back to Dallas and set our lives in order. We gave our notices at the church and seminary where we worked. We began to tell people that we were starting a church. The automatic question was, "Where?" We enthusiastically told them where God had called us. Yet, over and over again, we heard variations of, "You and every other Christian in the world!"

You would think that if a Christian wants to reach people with Christ's love, Christians would be excited or, at least, supportive. That, unfortunately, is seldom the case.

Nonetheless, God has called us here. So, on September 5, 1996, we loaded up everything and headed to the "Christian Mecca" of the world to reach the "sinners" unreached by the religious Christian community of Colorado Springs.

Halfway here, it dawned on me that we needed someone, preferably a strong male, to help us carry our heavy furniture up the thirteen steps of our second-story apartment.

And so, we prayed.

"Lord, we are going to Colorado Springs to start a church for You. Would You please allow us to meet someone who can help us move our furniture into our apartment? And Lord, can You make sure he is not a Christian? Amen."

We didn't *really* expect Him to answer the prayer request; after all, we would be arriving late at night.

When we finally got to the Springs, Tosha drove over to get the apartment keys from Melanie while I schemed in my mind how to get our king-sized mattress up the stairs so we would have something to sleep on for the night.

Exhausted from two days of driving, we had completely forgotten about our prayer request. But God did not!

I parked the U-haul, walked to the back of it, and opened it. Rummaging through our stuff, I tried to figure out how to get to that darn mattress, which, of course, was all the way in the front of the truck.

As I was pulling out boxes in desperate bid for a bed, a voice behind me asked, "Need some help?"

I turned in amazement to see not one but two able-bodied guys. It was a miracle. It was what I call "a microwave prayer" come true!

God was working on our behalf, and we were stunned.

God answers prayer. Can you believe it?

We exchanged introductions, my two answers to prayer and myself. Mark and Steve both appeared to have had plenty to drink that evening; I would even venture to say that Steve was drunk.

I noticed Mark was wearing a pair of shorts imprinted with the word "Seaside." We honeymooned in this romantic Florida town after we got married. We love Seaside, but we have seldom met people who know about it. So finding a complete stranger who had been there automatically gave us something in common.

I was spooked, but thankful to have someone help us find that mattress and get it inside for the evening. As the guys helped us move it up the stairs, Mark volunteered the two of them to help us move in the next day.

Later, as we finally lay our weary bodies to rest, we felt the slightest hope that just *maybe we had come to the right place.*

Too soon morning came, and I was knocking for some help. Mark, I quickly found out, could not help me because he had to go to work. "Steve will help you," he volunteered his friend. Unfortunately, Steve was, well ... recovering—if you know what I mean.

Eventually, though, he made his way over to help us. While we carried boxes up the steps to my office, we began to get to know each other. Steve was a military guy, visiting from Pensacola for a few weeks. He was getting out of the Navy soon and considering relocating to Colorado Springs.

During a pause in our conversation, Steve commented that we had a lot boxes all about the same size and quite heavy. Muscles aching, he asked, "What's in these?" "Books," I told him. "Who needs this many books?" Steve retorts.

Here it was: my opportunity to reach Steve for Jesus. All our hopes and dreams of evangelizing Colorado Springs quickly focused upon our first unwitting victim. Years later, Steve was going to make fun of me because of how intensely I went after him to be a part of the church. But, for today, he is just overwhelmed by us as we answer his questions.

"I am a pastor, and I came here to start a church."

He looks at me with puzzled eyes and says, "Start a church? I am Catholic. I thought churches were always around. You actually *start* them?"

He asked, so I told him everything. And, less than twelve hours after meeting the man, I closed the deal. "Would you like to be part of my church?'

Even as the words slipped out of my mouth, I sensed rejection close at hand. Steve shook his head, saying "I'm not much of a church person." Then, just as Mark had sacrificially offered him up to help us unload our furniture earlier that morning, Steve offered Mark up to the idea of going to church. "I'm not much of a church person, but I'm sure Mark would be."

Rejection! Doesn't it feel good? It makes us want to quit before we even get started. It makes us want to haul that mattress back down the stairs, shove it back in the truck, and retreat to the relative safety of what is familiar to us. It made us want to run back to Dallas as fast as we could.

Just because God had called us to Colorado Springs did not mean that we were not afraid. In fact, quite the opposite was true: we were shaking in our tennis shoes.

But God had broken our hearts for this city. He had opened doors and provided for us to be here. We could not run away, not yet. We had to press in, believing that He had called us.

Come to Colorado Springs!

Here we were, ready to be used but already suffering our first of many rejections.

Was there a point for us being here? In time, God will answer the question over and over again.

What's the POINT?

1. How is God breaking your heart for people?
2. What verses did God use to break you?
3. Has God answered a prayer you did not expect? Describe?

CHAPTER 2

Lord, Send People!

"Lord, send people!"

As I knelt in my apartment office just days after moving to Colorado Springs, I was scared to death.

How was I going to meet people?

How was I going to start a church?

How was I going to find people who did not have a relationship with Jesus Christ?

Lord, send people!

As I was earnestly praying, the doorbell rang, and it irritated me. Frustrated, I got up, went down a very long flight of steps, and opened the door. There stood a person who said, "Hello, my name is Lile. I'm here to fix your leaky pipes."

I had called the day before for a repair. I asked Lile to follow me back up the steps to where the leaky pipes were. Lile went to work on the pipes, and I went back to prayer in my makeshift office.

Lord, how do I meet people? Lord, send people!

Remember the story of the early church in Acts praying for Peter to get out of jail? It is recorded in Acts 12:5:

5 [W]hile Peter was in prison, the church prayed very earnestly for him.

No doubt the believers were praying for Peter to be released from prison. These were not just flippant, microwave prayers. These were *earnest* prayers, the God-we-desperately-need-Your-help sort of prayers.

Look what happened…

6 The night before Peter was to be placed on trial, he was asleep, chained between two soldiers, with others standing guard at the prison gate. 7 Suddenly, there was a bright light in the cell, and an angel of the Lord stood before Peter. The angel tapped him on the side to awaken him and said, "Quick! Get up!" And the chains fell off his wrists. 8 Then the angel told him, "Get dressed and put on your sandals." And he did. "Now put on your coat and follow me," the angel ordered. 9 So Peter left the cell, following the angel.

Can you believe that?

Peter escaped jail with a heavenly escort. God had totally answered the believers' prayers. You'd think they would immediately see God's hand at work. But look what happened next:

12 (Peter) went to the home of Mary, the mother of John Mark, where many were gathered for prayer. He knocked at the door in the gate, and a servant girl named Rhoda came to open it. 14 *When she recognized Peter's voice, she*

was so overjoyed that, instead of opening the door, she ran back inside and told everyone, "Peter is standing at the door!" 15 "You're out of your mind," they said. When she insisted, they decided, "It must be his angel." 16 Meanwhile, Peter continued knocking. When they finally went out and opened the door, they were amazed.

Guess I was not the only one who struggled to believe in the power of prayer!

Here I was in my makeshift office praying that God would send people. The doorbell rang, but I was annoyed by the interruption.

It never dawned on me that God was answering my prayer. I went down and opened the door. I talked to the person who was now standing in my bathroom just ten feet away from my office. I went back into my office, sat down, and began praying again for God to send people for me to meet.

I just didn't get it.

Why?

Because I didn't really believe God was going to answer prayer. Some people pray because that is what they are supposed to do; I just prayed because I didn't know what else to do.

A few minutes later, the person came out of the bathroom and interrupted my thick-headedness. "All done. I fixed your pipes." While I thanked Lile, it never dawned on me that this was a divine moment. Then, out of nowhere, Lile asked, "Why did you come to Colorado Springs?"

Suddenly, the light went on. I heard bells; I saw the sign. God penetrated the thickness of my mind and heart and removed the scales so I could see and feel that this was a divine moment. He had supernaturally orchestrated the answer to my prayer, and I was blown away.

After I gathered myself from being stunned by God's sovereignty, I answered, "My wife Tosha and I came here to start a church." And, eventually I get around to saying, "Next week we are starting an X-group on Tuesday night."

Lile asked me the question everybody since has asked, "What is an X-group?"

At Vanguard in those early days, an X-group was not a Bible study but a spiritual discussion group. In this non-threatening environment, people who did not profess to have a real relationship with Jesus could navigate through their questions about spirituality and God. If someone wanted our opinion, we shared our perspective based on what the Bible had taught us, but we were very careful not to give trite spiritual answers or to be judgmental toward those seeking truth. The most important aspect of an X-group was hearing an unbeliever's journey, giving them opportunity to express their struggles and pain, and talking about their spirituality.

"That sounds great," Lile responded. Then, after a pause he added, "I just recently lost my mother to cancer. I have a lot of questions about the afterlife and want to talk with someone about it."

There it was: the point of pain—the common ground we shared.

Just four years prior, I lost my own mother to a drunk driver. I was still as raw and broken over the loss of my mother as Lile was about the loss of his mother. We immediately connected.

Sharing that common ground, I invited Lile to be part of our X-group. After Steve's rejection of our church idea, I figured Lile would give me the same response. Wasn't I surprised! Lile assured me that he would come next Tuesday night and asked if he could bring his friend Jennifer.

"But of course," I responded.

Wow! I scored not just one but two participants for our first X-group! I was on cloud nine. I walked Lile out and marched back up the stairs to my makeshift office.

About this time, Tosha peeked in and inquired about our conversation. (Mind you, this was in the day when church-planting was so arduously slow that we actually had time to eavesdrop on each other then discuss what we heard in detail.)

I told Tosha about our maintenance person named Lile, about the loss of his mother and his interest in our upcoming X-group. "Plus," I add, "Lile is going to bring his girlfriend Jennifer next Tuesday."

Tosha quickly blew my bubble. "Um, Kelly," she said, with an odd look on her face, "I'm pretty sure that Lile is a 'she' not a 'he.'"

I gave Tosha a *What-is-wrong-with-you?* stare then proceeded to say, "Tosha, I think I know the difference between a man and a woman." I've got a graduate degree from seminary, for Pete's sake! Surely, recognizing the difference between the sexes is not too far beyond my capabilities!

That afternoon I learned the same painful lesson I have had to learn many times since in our marriage: my wife was right. I was wrong. Oh, those words cut deep.

Turned out Lile was indeed a woman. Lile was not her name, though. I had misheard her. She had said, "My name is Lil," short for 'Lillian.' But while she was not a man, Lil was a lesbian who invited her lover to come to X-group with us.

This was not exactly the way I envisioned starting a church. I grew up on a dairy farm in Kentucky. I knew more about dairy cows than I did about lesbian lovers. I was embarrassed by the misunderstanding and a bit freaked out.

I worried aloud to Tosha, "What am I going to do? I have invited a lesbian couple to our first X-group. What if they kiss? What if they ... whatever.... What do I do?" The tendency to be judgmental swelled up inside me.

I was scared to death, again.

What was I going to do? Should I back out of this? Should I uninvite them? I didn't approve of lesbians. I had never had a lesbian in my home much less a professing lesbian couple. This couldn't be God's will for this new church plant, could it?

Tosha and I prayed, reflecting on how Lil ended up at our door. We talked about how God sent Lil just as I was praying for God to send people. He must have wanted her to be part of our new church. But, never, ever, in my wildest dreams did I think we would start Vanguard with a lesbian couple.

We had been to Colorado Springs for less than a week. What relationships do we have to show for it? Two guys lit from bar hopping and two lesbian lovers.

Our church planting endeavor was off to a great start, right? What in the world are You up to, God?

"Lord, send people. I mean, Lord, send the people I want to reach. I guess I need to be more specific next time."

What's the POINT?

1. Has God ever answered your prayers in a way you didn't expect? Share an example and describe how it turned out.
2. How would you react if a woman came to your church whom you thought was a man?
3. Are you willing to interact with whomever God brings your way?

CHAPTER 3

The Same Old Story

In order to have a church, you have to have people.

One week after arriving to Colorado Springs, we knew exactly five: our college friend Melanie, our mattress-heaving buddies Steve and Mark, and our lesbian friends Lillian and Jennifer. At least two of the five were not so interested in church.

What were we going to do?

We had met a few other Christians, but most of them were not interested in what we were trying to do. They were looking for Bible studies rather than groups to help unbelievers process a relationship with the Lord. Their disinterest was disheartening, but we were not looking for a bunch of transplanted Christians to start a church with, anyway. We were looking for unbelievers after all, and we were desperate to find them.

Tosha and I decided to get up early every morning and go down to the workout room at our apartment complex. Surely that will be a good place to find unbelievers! Not so much. The room was full of equipment but empty of people.

Still, day after day we stuck with our routine, hoping something—someone—might come of it. Each morning we walked back to our apartment and ate breakfast while watching the early morning news on the local CBS affiliate station.

Somewhere along the way, we met this guy named Brian who was a Christian but who could not come to X-group because he had a bowling league on Tuesday nights. (Years later, this guy will turn out to be a beloved worship pastor at Vanguard. But, for now, he was just to us one more believer with a bunch of excuses as to why he couldn't be a part of helping us start a church.) Still Brian had lots of connections with people, and he started sending a few our way.

Eventually Brian talked us into starting a Sunday night X-group so he could attend. Since he had a plethora of friends, we agreed. Shortly after this, I got a phone call.

Now, the phone did not ring much during these painful early days of church planting. Each phone call was like a miracle. I answered the call with baited breath.

"Hello, this is Kelly."

The voice on the other end of the line said, "Hello, this is Susan. I am friends with Tina, who is good friends with Brian. Brian told Tina to tell me that I should call you guys and see if you can help me." Susan paused, then continued describing herself. "I am going through a difficult time in my life and I need someone to talk to about spirituality. Would you be willing to talk with me?"

I was thinking, *Are you kidding? Of course I'm willing!* but I more graciously responded, "Sure."

Susan asked, "When can we meet?"

I replied, "How about today?" (After all, all Tosha and I had—besides a calling from God and a lot of fear—was time on our hands.)

A few hours later, the doorbell rang. We opened the door and our jaws dropped. Here at our front door stood one of the CBS early morning show anchors.

I was stunned, again. The words, "We watch you every morning," managed to fall out of my mouth as we invited Susan up the stairs.

What little did we know that the next "victim" of our feeble evangelistic efforts would be found not in the apartment complex weight room but at our front door. She came to us through the most unlikely possible means, and we had watched her on TV for days.

We could hardly believe our little church plant of six or seven people had such a celebrity in its midst.

Tosha and I sat down at the kitchen table with Susan and talked.

She immediately opened up to us. After sharing a bit of her story, she said, "My life is falling apart. I don't know what to do."

I probed, "Do you pray?"

Susan admitted she usually read her horoscope and occasionally consulted fortunetellers. "Sometimes I go outside and look for signs in the stars," she told us. "I consider myself a stargazer."

My seminary training kicked in and I asked, "Susan, do you have a Bible?" When Susan shook her head, I asked her, "If I get you a Bible, will you read it?" She assured us she would read it, but she told us she did not know where or what to read.

After grabbing her a Bible from my office, I said, "Read the Gospel of John," as I showed her where the book was located. "When you read this, I want you to say to God, 'If You are real, make Your Son Jesus Christ real to me.'"

Incredulously, Susan looked up from the pages and said, "I didn't know Jesus is God. I thought Christians made that up."

I could not help but laugh. I did not know this experience was possible in "Christian" America. I said, "No, Susan, Jesus actually *said* He is God."

Dumbfounded, Susan replied, "Really, I never knew that. I just thought Christians made that up to get you to go to church."

After a long conversation, we prayed with Susan, then she went back out into her world to find out if Jesus Christ was really God and if He would be real to her.

About a week later, we met with Susan again. She became a regular at our Sunday night X-group. We became friends.

Eventually the three of us sat down to follow up on our first conversation. I asked her, "What did you think about the Gospel of John?"

"I really liked it," she said, then she added that she had read Matthew, Mark, and Luke, too.

"But, I just don't get it," she continued in a perplexed tone.

"Get what?" Tosha asks.

"Well, after reading John, I read Matthew, Mark and Luke, too. But they're the same damn story. What's that all about?" She just did not understand why the Bible is redundant.

Tosha and I were so taken aback at Susan's assessment that we about fell on the floor laughing. Our Bible college and seminary educations did not prepare us for this response to the Gospel. Susan's naiveté took us completely by surprise, but we attempted to give her childlike question a meaningful answer.

Over and over again, God woos us to Himself. Over and over again, His Word expresses His love for people. The Gospels tell the same story from different angles in order to reach different groups of people. Susan seemed satisfied with our response.

Later, as I thought about Susan's reaction and got past my chuckles over her description of the Gospels, I began to realize that I had more in common with Susan than I originally thought. When it comes to God, I just don't get it, either. I came to Colorado

Springs with my plan for how I was going to plant a church, and I was continually disappointed when it did not go as I planned.

Yet, over and over again God was wooing not just unbelievers but also *me* to Himself. Over and over again He expressed His love for me by providing, by answering prayer, by sovereignly orchestrating events.

Humbled, I fell on my knees in worship. The Gospels were not just the same story told in redundant fashion. The Gospels were the heart of God trying to reach my heart.

That is the point of evangelism, something that even a bona fide, certified Southern Baptist church planter needed to be reminded of.

Over and over again, God shows thick-headed Christians like me the power of the Gospel. It changes lives: it changed mine, and it eventually changed Susan's.

But that's another story.

READ one of the Gospels, asking God to help you read it as if for the first time.

What's the POINT?

1. Does it seem miraculous that Susan showed up at our door?
2. Have you ever had someone show up unexpectedly in your life, asking you for spiritual direction? How did this come about? What happened?
3. Do you have a Susan in your life now? What is this person's story? How are you encouraging this person?

CHAPTER 4

A Lesbian Couple

"Um, hello. My name is Denise. I heard on the radio that Kelly and Tosha are starting a church called Vanguard, and I was wondering, are you a lesbian couple?"

How should I respond to this one? Is it a trick? Will a "no" answer be a relief to Denise or a turnoff? What in the world made her ask if we were lesbian?

The possibilities squirmed through my mind as I responded with, "Why do you ask?" Denise replied assertively, "Because I am a goddess worshipper. I want to be around people who value women and show respect and value to women."

I laughed. "Well, Denise, I am Kelly. And, as you can tell by my voice, I am not a woman and, as far as I know, I've never been a woman. However, I want you to know I greatly value women. I believe that it's important that we do not treat women like second-class citizens."

It was the spring of 1997, and Vanguard had had public worship services for a few months now. God was sending us people; in fact, He sent almost a hundred for our first service, thanks to some radio advertising.

Of course, more than one church and local pastor had raised their brows at our cutting-edge methods of serving lattes and lighting candles during services. A decade later, these methods would be the norm for churches, but, for now, these were a little too edgy for some.

Also, it probably did not help how we were perceived in the Christian community that we called our services "R-rated." This was a totally logical name, fully in keeping with the movie-theater theme we started with. To our thinking, "X-groups" — where people can discuss their spirituality in safety and even anonymity — were logically followed with "R-rated-services" — where people can come build relationship with God and others. The "R" stands for "relationship" as well as "REAL." This would become our theme as a church.

Made perfect sense to us, and we advertised accordingly.

However, many people, like Denise, thought we were a lesbian couple who had started a naked church. Rumors both in the believing and unbelieving community spread about us. The unbelieving community thought we were a lesbian couple who worshiped in the nude, and the believing community thought we were a cult. (When you attempt to love unbelieving people, you quickly find yourself in no man's land, literally and figuratively.)

Still, Vanguard caught Denise's attention. She was scared, broken, bewildered, and trying to find God — even though she did not realize it right then. To our surprise, even though we weren't a lesbian couple and didn't practice goddess worship, Denise decided to attend Vanguard's church services and join an X-group. Thus began a new relationship for Tosha and I.

Denise eventually admitted that our names were what initially intrigued her enough to inquire about Vanguard. And, once she decided to engage with our growing church community, she felt loved and valued, not just as a woman but as a person.

Denise felt like we would accept her even if we disagreed with her. Little could she know that being this kind of person did not come naturally to me, but this was how God was teaching me to lead others to Him.

In an interview early on in Vanguard's existence, Denise said this:

> "People are looking for the kind of environment where they can express their questions about God or question His existence or even ask questions about evolution. They want a safe environment where they're not going to be judged for having different points of view. I was looking for these things, too.

> "I was going through a really bad time in my life—it was right after college and I wasn't connecting with anyone or finding a job that I liked, and things were just getting really bad. I got to the point where I'd try anything—Buddhism, Native American religions, goddess worship—and I tried all those things, but they didn't take away the *pain* in my life.

> "I prayed to God to reveal Himself to me, and I started praying every night. Shortly after that, I heard an ad on secular radio for Vanguard Church. I called and talked with Kelly for about twenty minutes. I basically said that the church sounded too good to be true. I didn't have to dress up, and they had a coffee-house mentality there. I asked him, 'Do you have to be a Christian to come?' He said, 'No. Wherever you are in your spiritual journey, you're welcome here.'

"I was really shocked by that. The churches that I had gone to—I had never thought I could ask that or just walk in the door and not be a Christian and still come to church.

"I almost talked myself out of going, because I thought, *It has to be a cult or something weird.* When I went, at first I thought that people were being nice to me so they could get me to come to Christ faster, but there was really no pressure from anyone. They gave me my space to explore and let God intervene."

And, God does intervene. Just when Denise thought she was looking for some goddess-worshipping, R-rated lesbian pastors, God was looking for her. He found her, and she found Him. What an amazing time it was when Denise gave her heart to the Lord!

The Bible shows that God uses everything to draw people to Himself. He used a donkey in the Old Testament, tongues, a murderer, and even a false idol in the New Testament.

The apostle Paul said he became all things to all people in order to win some.

Denise was afraid to reach out and come to regular church. But when, through radio, we reached out to her, she was willing to interact. Our name, of all things, was what first struck a cord with her. God uses anything and everything to get people's attention. God even gave me the name He did so Denise would be interested in Him. All my life I've taken flak about my name being a girl's name. (It is an Irish *male* name that means *warrior*, by the way.) But it ended up being the very thing God used to draw Denise to Himself. Yeah, "Kelly and Tosha" didn't turn out to be lesbians, but, in the end, that didn't matter. Doesn't God have a sense of humor?

It is so easy to be an inward-focused Christian. It is easy to be wrapped up in a Bible study or small Christian cell group. It is natural to care for people who believe like you do.

But God wants us to stretch ourselves. He wants us to take risks and reach out. I believe that risk involves three primary things: your time, money, and heart. Do you invest time in a thriving community of believers that is going after the "goddess" worshippers of your day? Do you give of your financial resources so that the Denises of the world can hear about the love of Jesus Christ through radio advertising—even if that is on secular radio? Is your heart invested in the ministry of reaching "sinners" with the Gospel?

If not, why? Do you care? If not, why not? If so, what are you doing about it?

Sometimes Christians say to me, "I am praying that God will give me a burden for the lost." That, I tell them, is a good start. But it is only the start.

The only way I have learned to get a burden for the lost is to spend time with them, to look into their eyes, to hear their voices, and to care about the stories of their lives. These moments are often uncomfortable, especially when you are mistaken for somebody else like I was with Denise or when you totally put your foot in your mouth like I did with Lil. It is never easy to go outside your safety zone, whether it means leaving a city to go plant a church where you don't know anybody or going across the street to meet a neighbor with different political views.

Nonetheless, these moments are pivotal for the Kingdom. And we must be prepared to engage them, even when they come enwrapped with strange questions. Ready to have your personal identity mistaken in order for someone to meet the most important Person in the universe?

Your phone is ringing. Who knows? It might be a goddess worshipper mistakenly wondering who you are.

What's the POINT?

1. When was the last time an unbeliever contacted you? Your church?
2. Are you willing to be mistaken by the "Denises" of the world in order to reach some of them with the love of Jesus Christ?
3. What are some things you can do to reach out to unbelievers in your life? Maybe you don't know any. Begin right now asking God to give you opportunities and ideas to reach people in His name.

CHAPTER 5

Making Cookies

"Daddy, God told me to make our neighbors some cookies."

Vanguard Church is about five years old at this time. Tosha and I were no longer a couple of twenty-ish people without kids. We had two daughters by this time with a son on the way. As our family had grown, Vanguard had, too. Since those tiny beginning X-groups in our apartment, we had connected with hundreds of people, hired staff members, and even purchased an old movie theater to meet in.

We were a regular, bona fide church now. The point of evangelism sometimes gets lost in the shuffle of staff issues, budget meetings, and incorporating people, though.

What's the point, anyway? Really, I *know* evangelism is God's calling on my life, but sometimes I just can't keep up with it.

Anyway, early this morning four-year old Anastasha wakened me with the revelation she was given in her sleep last night. Just as with little Samuel in the Old Testament, God spoke to Anastasha in her sleep, and she awoke from her dream compelled to serve her neighbors.

Frankly, I was a bit concerned about Anastasha's enthusiasm. You see, our neighborhood was not very friendly. Our neighbors seemed very closed off to us; one of our neighbors wouldn't even look at us when we waved to her as she backed out of her driveway each morning. We wondered if we had done something to offend her. Or, maybe she just did not like us because she was old while we were young and had noisy children. Maybe it was because she knew I was a pastor. (That news always seemed to travel pretty fast in the neighborhood.)

We didn't know why this particular neighbor did not seem to like us. Whatever the reason, we were a little concerned about the possible rejections that Anastasha might experience from our neighbors. But, oh well, we let her move ahead with her cookie endeavor because we had the uncanny feeling that God was behind it.

Since Anastasha was only four, Tosha did most of the cookie making. This, however, did not deter Anastasha's enthusiasm. All through the process we tried to downplay the potential responses she might get from the neighbors, but nothing deterred her. She was determined to make our neighbors happy and be obedient to what God had told her to do.

Toward day's end, cookie-making process complete, Tosha and I stood out in the driveway as Anastasha walked the cookies to each house. She made them for four families. She started two houses down; she rang the doorbell but got no answer. She went across the street; again, she rang the doorbell but got no answer. Then Anastasha went to our next-door neighbor to the east; she rang the doorbell and got no answer. At each home, she just left the cookies inside the storm doors with a note.

We thought she might be discouraged and disappointed but nothing seemed to stifle her excitement and desire to serve our neighbors. She was on a mission from God, and nothing was going to stop her.

Finally, Anastasha approached her final home. She walked up to the home of our neighbor to the west, the neighbor who rarely smiled when we waved to her. Because of the position of the front door compared to our driveway, we couldn't see Anastasha as she rang the doorbell. The garage blocked our ability to see their front door, so we were unsure what was going on.

A few eternal moments later, Anastasha strolled out like a four-year old who just changed someone's life by performing the greatest God act of her life. No, not really. She sauntered over to our yard with a casual look.

We asked, "Was Mrs. Judy at home?"

She said, "Yes."

"Did you give her the cookies?"

A nonchalant answer came forth. "Yes."

"Well, what did she say?" we pressed, trying to get a few details out of our reticent preschooler.

Anastasha replied, "She said thank you then started crying."

Anastasha strolled off into our house while Tosha and I stood in the driveway wondering, "Why did she cry? They're just cookies."

A few months passed. Occasionally I saw Judy's husband out in the yard doing this or that. He was quiet but pleasant, a retired Air Force officer in his mid-fifties. Sometimes I said hi, and we carried on small talk.

But I had no idea, though, what was really going on in my neighbors' lives.

Then one day the doorbell rang. I went to the door expecting yet another solicitor. Instead, the person on my porch brought grim news. "Judy asked me to come over and tell you that Jim died yesterday."

It was like a ton of bricks were launched at my heart all at once.

The person told me that Jim had bone cancer which had been in remission for years but had just recently come back with a vengeance. He went into the hospital and was dead within days.

Dumbfounded, I closed my door. How could I have been so insensitive and unaware? How could I have been so concerned about being rejected by my neighbor not to find out why she rarely smiled? Why didn't I follow up with her and see why the cookies made her cry? Why was I so insensitive that I didn't even know my neighbor was sick, much less, dying?

Why? Because I didn't know what was going on in their lives and, honestly, I am not sure I truly cared.

Don't all of us Christians and followers of Jesus Christ have seasons and times when we just want to be left alone? Sometimes we have lifetimes like this. We want our space, and we want others to have their space. We want to do "nice" things for people when God wakes our four-year-olds up to make cookies, but we don't genuinely want to be bothered by the problems and struggles of the unbelieving world.

I can't believe I was so insensitive. Like old Eli in Samuel's day, it did not dawn on me that God had something to say to me until He awakened a child to bring me the message. But, even in the midst of Anastasha's enthusiasm, I ignored His prompting.

Soon after the knock on my door, I found myself sitting in a funeral home and participating in the funeral of a next-door neighbor who, quite frankly, I didn't even know. I knew how his grass was doing and how his trees were growing, but I did not know the first thing about the man's story. And now he was gone.

I am reminded of my need to listen to the voice of God, respond to what He tells me to do, and look for ways to get to know those He has placed around me.

Our next-door neighbors are neither accidents nor coincidences. We may not like them or even choose them as our neighbors, but—like family members—they have been chosen for us. Chosen, really? By whom? I believe by God. Subdivisions seldom afford us much privacy, and we often look for every possible way to get a private moment to ourselves. This can be really important for surviving the rat races of our lives. Yet, at the same time, we have a mandate to share the story of how Jesus has redeemed our lives.

I missed it when God was prompting me in my neighbor's life. I ignored what He was doing around me. But I learned a lesson I hope never to forget.

Next time one of my children says, "Daddy, God wants me to make cookies for our neighbors," I will give a different response. *Good!*

"God, what do You want *me* to do?"

READ the story of Philip in Acts 8:26–40 being called to go share the Gospel with the Ethiopian Eunuch.

What's the Point?

1. What keeps you from caring for your neighbors?
2. Do you remember the first time God ever spoke to you?
3. Describe the first time you felt a burden to help someone in a way that was out of the ordinary for your life.

CHAPTER 6

Community Discussions

What does the Bible have to say about homosexuality?

The spring of 2004 was full and weighty when I was invited with a group of local pastors to a pastors' breakfast at Focus on the Family. The head of a pro-gay activist group was coming to town and demanded a meeting with Dr. Dobson, the founder of Focus. Dr. Dobson was informed that if he did not meet with the activist, Focus would be picketed to the point of complete disruption. Dr. Dobson refused the meeting but, instead, asked Colorado Springs pastors to come meet with him to discuss the issue of homosexuality.

Every church in America faces this issue. How do we talk to gays? Even more pressing, what do we do with people who believe it is okay to be gay yet want something to do with the church?

Colorado Springs' approach has been to stand at a distance and shoot. The left shoots the right, then the right shoots back, usually using the media to convey our deep-felt beliefs and opinions of how people ought to live and treat one another. We buy media rights and blast one another from a distance. This seems to be effective ... at least, effective enough to create explosions. The collateral damage is more than the Church should be willing to pay, but we often do not consider that. Christians just blast away for the sake of what we believe is right.

Over the years, I have watched the right and left of Colorado Springs attack one another over the issues of abortion, gay marriage, the environment, and more. While this sort of approach is sometimes necessary, the more we move into a post-god, post-church society in the United States and across the world, this strategy is becoming less and less effective for believers. Vanguard desires to find a new way to engage an old argument.

I have no problem with strong stances on moral issues. I believe we have a mandate from God to be committed to the moral issues of our day and to live out these convictions. But, with that said, how do we go about it?

In the spring of 2004, many ideas are floating around for staving off the attack of the liberals. Many of these ideas would not contribute to building relationship with unbelievers. Instead, they would just push people further away from us.

So, at that pastors' meeting at Focus, I raised my hand and asked to share my thoughts when given the opportunity. Dr. Dobson acknowledged me and allowed me to speak. I knew I needed to establish my credentials before sharing deep convictions about this subject.

I told Dr. Dobson that I grew up listening to him on the radio just like so many others had. I had deep respect for him and appreciated his years of integrity in leading our city, country and world. I told Dr. Dobson I graduated from Liberty University under the leadership of his friend, Dr. Jerry Falwell. I married my college sweetheart, then we moved to Dallas to attend Dallas

Theological Seminary, where I studied under the presidential leadership of Dr. Chuck Swindoll, another of his trusted friends.

I reassured Dr. Dobson and the other pastors that I was as conservative as they came in my theology. But—I take a deep breath—I suggested that it was time for us to try some new approaches in order to demonstrate what it looked like to be a "friend of sinners" as Jesus was.

I proposed that Colorado Springs have a community discussion and invite both sides to the table. We needed to bring the issues out of the public arena into a private setting where we could add names and faces to the issues. The only way to get a burden for the lost is to spend time with them. A community discussion would enable us to do this. We could begin to build real relationship with the community by showing love, respect, and dignity to people even while disagreeing with them. Everyone deserves this because we are created in the image of God. Regardless of our position or stance on issues, I say *we firmly believe that we can't influence people if we are not in relationship with them.*

Dr. Dobson asked me if I believe and teach that homosexuality is a sin. Both of these I do. However, I added, "Homosexuality is *a* sin but not *the* sin." Dr. Dobson then asked me, "Do you have children?" I had four young children at the time. He looked at me as if I were an enigma then moved on to other questions. I didn't know what to think except that he must have not liked my idea, so I sat the rest of the meeting in silence.

After the meeting was over, one of the leaders of Focus on the Family asked for my cell number. Later that day, Tom Minnery called saying that the gender department of Focus would like to meet with me and see if this community discussion idea could work.

So Vanguard and Focus worked together to try something new: engaging the "other side" in Colorado Springs, instead of just shooting at them. Focus prepared and filled the discussion panel with three leaders opposed to gay marriage; I identified three speakers to address this issue from a pro-gay perspective, including Christians who did not believe that homosexuality is a sin. There was a pastor, the interim leader of the Pikes Peak Gay and Lesbian Center, and a chaplain of a local college.

The night of our big event turned into a media frenzy as our city came together *in our church* to discuss the divisive issue of homosexuality. About twelve hundred people were present for this electrifying evening. The media was stumped by our civility toward one another. Gay couples came in holding hands just as straight couples do. Conservatives sat next to cross-dressers; gay activists sat next to soccer moms. Polarizing beliefs charged the atmosphere as I moderated the discussion between the two sides of the panel.

What's the point in doing this?

There is one reason and one reason only: to be a friend of sinners like Jesus.

To the world the Church is not only irrelevant, it is downright offensive. People—gays included—are spiritual; they are often even interested in Jesus. But their view of church and religion is becoming increasingly negative with every passing year. The judgmental spirit of religion interwoven with the hypocrisy of religious leaders leaves us with baggage greater than the world can endure or desire. We have lost our way in loving the lost because we are sidetracked with fear that they might get an upper hand on us regarding certain moral issues in our day.

However, on this brisk fall evening, our city was welcomed into the church—and the city came. A respectful discussion between both sides took place. Focus demonstrated incredible compassion and grace for the people across the aisle even as they articulated the biblical view that homosexuality is a sin. The night was amazing; years later we did this event again with the current President of Focus on Family, Jim Daly, a dear friend.

The tide and temperature of our city began turning this evening. As we laid down our semiautomatic media machine guns, we came to the table and talked like sensible people. We actually listened to one another, heard one another. And Christians learned to love the *people* we meet more than our good, godly *opinions* about them.

Something amazing happens when Christians replace fear and judgment with relationship. We cannot change our view of people if we don't get to know them. We cannot influence people if we are not in relationship with them. And we cannot effect change in our society if we refuse to listen to anyone who doesn't agree with everything we say.

Jesus never shouted at "sinners"; instead, He engaged them in relationship. The only times Jesus ever got angry were when religiously hypocritical, judgmental people got in the way of others experiencing God. And sometimes, we must admit, we as Christians do this.

It is time for us to start getting the point of evangelism — befriending sinners like Jesus!

Jesus loves people. He died for them — *all* of them, including the ones who have political and moral beliefs that run counter to His Word.

People begin to experience His love when they experience our love. Seems a mighty high calling to love the "other side" when we so thoroughly disagree with them. Yet, this is what His Word calls us to do. It is an overwhelming challenge when we look at it from the big picture perspective. But, really, it starts quite simply: with relationship.

We love people when we begin to look at the whites of their eyes, hear their stories, and care about them. Such an approach is worlds away from blasting those who are on the opposite side of the aisle.

What's the POINT?

1. Do you look for ways to relate to unbelievers around you, or do you tend to isolate yourself from them?
2. How does your church fight the judgmental religious spirit in your city?
3. What risks do you take to reach out to people who are different from you?

CHAPTER 7

Realize the Cost

The religious of Jesus' day called him "the friend of sinners,"; they meant it as an insult, he took it as a compliment.

He got this title because he spent so much time loving people that the religious community refused to even associate with, much less socialize with.

Jesus didn't just socialize with them, he loved them. He loved them regardless of what it cost him.

We have been challenged by Jesus' example to live the same. Maybe this overwhelms you and creates a sense of confusion, chaos, and fear in your Christianity. Maybe deep down if you are honest with yourself, "loving sinners" and being a "friend of sinners" is not something you feel very comfortable with in your religious life.

Let us encourage you by saying that we understand. We felt the same way once upon a time. However, loving people should not be so overwhelming, but sometimes we get stumped in the practical application of it.

When we came to Colorado Springs in 1996 to start Vanguard, Tosha and I set out with the motto of *loving people into a REAL relationship with Jesus Christ*. Great motto, one that countless people have resonated with and memorized. Even young children have taken up this banner for purpose in their lives.

Still, we have struggled to know exactly *how* to live it. What does it mean to have REAL relationship? How do we *love* people into that?

These are the questions we asked and tried to answer for over a decade of Vanguard's existence. Though we wanted our church plant to be perfect, we never achieved that—even in something as foundational as knowing exactly how to live out our mission. Still, peoples' lives were being affected and changed through loving, nonjudgmental relationships with Christians. So we knew we were on to something, and we kept asking the question.

In the early days, Tosha and I joked that REAL was an acronym for "Relationally Enthusiastic About Life." Now, there's some deep stuff for which to sacrifice everything. (No, not really.) REAL had to mean something more, something so much more, if it was going to effect true change in peoples' lives. Not only that, REAL had to mean something more than our society's current obsession with puking out emotions on unwitting individuals for the sake of being known. Vanguard tried that approach, too, with little positive impact. Vulnerability, in and of itself, does not show love or make you feel loved.

Slowly, through the stories surfacing at Vanguard, we began to see a pattern of relationship that epitomized REAL. And we did create an acronym worthy of remembering—and living.

How do you *love people into a REAL relationship with Jesus Christ?* Four ways:

1. Realize the Cost
2. Embrace His Commands

3. Align Your Allegiance
4. Love Others like Jesus

As Christians sincerely trying to walk with the Lord, we most often jump straight to number four, the "love" part. This is good, noble and right, but we get frustrated and sometimes even lose our way in loving when the unexpected comes our way.

In the next four chapters, I am going to briefly walk you through what it means to have a real relationship with Jesus Christ.

When Jesus laid the foundation of the church, He told the disciples this about being in relationship with Him:

> If you want to be my follower you must love me *more* than your own father, and mother, wife and children, brothers and sisters—yes, *more* than your own life. Otherwise, you *cannot* be my disciple. And you *cannot* be my disciple if you do not *carry* your own cross and *follow* me.
>
> *But don't begin until you count the cost.* For who would begin construction of a building without first getting estimates and then checking to see if there is enough money to pay the bills?... No one can become my disciple without giving up *everything* for me.
>
> Luke 14:26–28, 33

Now, you might want to stop right here. You may want to put this book down and just keep doing things the way you've always done them. If you keep reading, you may find that your perceptions about evangelism are going to be challenged. You are going to learn things from here on that may cost you your career, marriage, relationships, family, money, house, even your very life. If you live what you read from this point on, it may cost you *everything.*

But here it is: *you and I must love God more than we love our own lives.*

You see, being a dedicated, sold-out Christ-follower does not start with evangelism and loving everybody to Jesus. (I know. Alarms are probably going off in your head saying I am a heretic. But stick with me here.)

Being a Christ-follower starts, first, with loving God most and counting the cost to follow Him in loving everybody else.

This is how real relationship starts with God—and then continues with other people. You must **realize the cost**, meaning experience the cost.

You and I don't know what it will cost to follow God. When we make our commitment to be His, we have no idea how much will be required of us. We just need to be willing to pay whatever price is required. The cost is *everything.* Everything? *Everything.*

In my life, there have been days when I did not think my relationship with God was worth it. There have been many times when loving unbelievers just didn't seem worth it, either.

The cost is often high; the sacrifice is sometimes outrageous. The faith required is greater than I can muster.

I'm sure you experience this, too.

But here we are looking at the very costs which Jesus calls us to take into account from the very beginning of our walk with Him.

Are you willing to risk your life to save another? Are you willing to expose your life, all of it if necessary to save another? Are you willing to die so others can experience a real relationship with Jesus Christ? Good, then all I am going to ask you to do in the remainder of this book is to live for Him. (Sometimes dying for Him is easier than actually living for Him, by the way.)

I want to challenge you to *realize the cost* by risking for others who do not have a real relationship with Jesus Christ.

When our church hosts community discussions, I expect to take hits from the unbelieving world. You get a room full of people with polarized beliefs and the atmosphere is charged with every emotion imaginable. Honestly I have anticipated guns, knives or, at least, vicious words from the "other side." I expect high costs from those who believe different than me.

The costs I did not expect, though, were the personal attacks from within the church. People who say they follow Christ have risen up against me when I risked reaching others for Christ. Each time Vanguard risked for the outsiders of our city, we took hits from the religious community.

Not until our community discussion on "Would Jesus Go Green?" had we taken hits from the religious community inside our own church, though.

For this event, we partnered with my friend who owns the leading liberal newspaper of our city. He invited a leading evangelical from Washington involved with the National Association of Evangelicals to come speak at the event. Vanguard opened its doors to the community and shared the platform with the outsiders of our city on this issue.

We did this because we care about the environment but, more importantly because we care about relationships. We want to build relationships with "outsiders." We want the city to see our church as a place they are welcome to come and talk about the issues that affect all of our lives, whether we are inside or outside the church.

I believe that you can't influence *"sinners"* if you are not *in* relationship with them. And you cannot be in relationship with them if you can't find some sort of common ground.

You do not have to agree with people on every moral issue in order to partner with them on the ones you do. But many

Christians think they have to agree with everything in order to agree on anything. Other Christians think that if you agree on one thing, then you give the perception that you agree on everything. This simply is not true.

My city is very politically divided. We have the extreme right and the extreme left. I have often wondered why we as Christians partner with those on the right of the political aisle, even if they don't believe Jesus is God, while, at the same, we refuse relationship with our brothers and sisters in Christ who believe people should have a choice on abortion and a right to choose homosexuality.

Now, for the record, Vanguard is pro-life and pro-family. We believe that these are moral issues that God addresses in Scripture.

However, why is it against the "religious rules" to partner with pro-gay Christians but we can partner with other faiths in our city who are pro-life and anti-Jesus?

Make sense to you? It doesn't to me, unless, of course, politics matter more than the Gospel! Ah, now we are getting somewhere! Do you feel a little rise in the temperature right now? I do!

But now we are taking inventory. Are we more afraid of people being gay or of them being godly? Are we more concerned that people choose life or that they choose Jesus?

I fully realize that this is a bed of hot coals I'm walking on right now. But think about it with me. We, Christians, partner with the necessary political machines to stomp out immorality while we let the rejection of Jesus become a secondary issue to us. Welcome to twenty-first century American political Christianity! We unite over politics and moral issues, but we refuse to talk to brothers and sisters who believe Jesus is God but still embrace homosexuality.

Now, I am not saying that churches that utilize the "don't ask, don't tell" policy need to be pro-gay. We believe the Bible teaches that homosexuality is a sin, but it is *a* sin not *the* sin.

However, we have learned in Colorado Springs that you don't mess with its religious reputation or you will have the demons of religion unleashed on you. We have the marks upon our spiritual souls to prove it.

So we had a community discussion and invited the "sinners" to join us on "Would Jesus Go Green?" Some of those sinners are pro-choice and pro-gay; all of us are pro-environment. (Regardless of whether global warming is primarily caused by humans or we contribute to it or it's not happening at all, we believe God wants us to provide Creation care and not waste the resources He has entrusted to us.)

Well, you would think I invited the church to join the devil for a study on how to convert believers to Satanism. The comments fired at me were blistering.

How dare you bring those worldly institutions into our church!
Those people have no right to be here!
If you want to reach them, go for it. But leave us out of it!

It seems as if you can have a bad marriage, get divorced, commit adultery, leave your spouse, and can still be restored to the church to lead again. However, if you are gay, going green or Democrat, you are screwed. You are lower than the low. Sinners!

I had never been attacked by people who attended my church when we sought to reach out into the community but this time I was, and I paid a high price for it. If I tried to build bridges to bring "sinners" in, my reputation, my ministry, my own personal integrity might be raked over the coals.

Even in my own church, there are people who could care less if we reach "sinners." They don't want "sinners" coming into our church except to repent. They don't want "sinners" having a voice at our church except to say they are sorry for being such horrible people. They don't want them having any place in our lives or church until they have repented. *Then* the former "sinners" are welcome. (If this is your thought process, then good luck! Enjoy your infatuation with your self-righteousness. You will be rich in your opinions but extremely poor in relationship.)

I am determined to *realize the cost* and fight against this.

Vanguard is a church where people of all opinions are welcome. We do this by more than simply putting the "all welcome" letters out on the marquis; we look for and create common ground. We desire the opportunity, through realizing the cost and taking a risk in relationship with them, to love "sinners" into a real relationship with Jesus Christ.

We want Vanguard to be known as a church that is "a friend of sinners" like Jesus regardless of the cost.

And one way we have done this as a church is by inviting both sides of a discussion into our four walls. We give equal time to each perspective and allow opportunity for people to respond. We state the truth of Scripture, and we respectfully hear others speak their opinions.

We are not pro-gay or pro-choice; we are pro-relationship with "sinners."

You can't influence people if you are not in relationship with them.

I have been told that if I want to make a name for my church in Colorado Springs, I should learn to partner with more "respectable" Christian organizations. And we do, but that is just half of the equation. We believe that churches should also look for ways to invite the civic portions of their city into their facilities and be hosts to them and demonstrate to them the love of Jesus Christ through building relationship with them.

This does not require the traditional revival service where you invite an evangelist to come and preach fire and brimstone and get the same people saved again. It can be as simple as having a topic of discussion and inviting people from the right and left of an issue to come to your church for a community forum. You will need to agree in advance on some common rules, and you will probably need someone who can serve as an impartial moderator. As you show love and respect to people as you respectfully disagree with them, you will add a name and face to the issue. You might be amazed at how God replaces your fear with love. You might be amazed how much of a burden you get for the "sinner."

Over the years, people have said to me, "I would reach the lost if God would just give me a burden for them." Well, let me tell you that God will give you the burden for the "sinner" when you look into the whites of their eyes and listen to their stories and become a friend to them. As you hear where they are coming from, you know what? You will have to *realize the cost.* Your relationship with them will certainly cost you something.

It will more than likely cost you things like ... your religious reputation, self-righteous pride, and your preconceived opinions of others.

It may even cost you your political beliefs, as important as those are.

Your relationship with God will cost you. Your relationship with others in His name will cost you, too. But nothing matters more to God than the souls of humans. Nothing!

Maybe it will cost you everything, like Jesus!

How about you? Is it worth it to you?

Is it worth the cost to be a "friend of sinners"?

Jesus decided, "Yes."

We hope you do, too.

That is the first step to *becoming a friend of sinners like Jesus.*

Read Luke 9:57–62

What's the POINT?

1. What does realizing the cost mean to you when it comes to reaching the lost?
2. Do you believe that you have to agree with people on every moral issue in order to partner with them? Why or why not?
3. A community discussion may not be the way for your church to go about engaging your city, but what are some other ways you can do this?

CHAPTER 8

Embrace His Commands

If you love me, obey my commandments.

Who said it? Your parent? Your big brother? Your school teacher? Your boss?

Yes!

And his name is Jesus. He is your spiritual parent, spiritual big brother, spiritual school teacher, and your boss.

He wants you to obey Him.

But what we miss is we think that He wants us to obey Him and then He will love us.

No, He already loves us.

Romans 5:8 tells us, "But God showed his great love for us by sending Christ to die for us *while we were still sinners.*"

There is nothing you can do in the rest of your life to make God love you more than He already does.

He loves you.

He doesn't want you to obey Him so He will love you. He wants you to obey Him because that shows that you love Him.

Why is that? Because He knows how much we love sin and disobedience. It is our nature. It is our nature to disobey and embrace this world's principles instead of Him.

He wants you and me to *embrace his commands*.

And He wants you and me to be motivated by love to do it.

So much of Christianity unfortunately is motivated by religion. It is motivated by a man-centered approach by getting people to do what other people want them to do through guilt, manipulation, and fear. God wants you to do what you do out of love. Why? Because that is why He did what He did for us.

While we were sinners ... God showed his great love for us by sending Christ to die for us....

So much of evangelism is often motivated out of guilt, manipulation, and fear that one day the blood of other human beings will be on our hands. We are guilted into evangelizing others. This is not God's plan. God wants us to be motivated out of love for Him and pursue others like He pursues us.

Why? Because it is God's love that changed you, and it is God's love flowing through you that is really going to change others.

Do you love the lost? Do you love the "sinner"?

Jesus did.

What motivated Him to do what He did for us was love.

He wants a relationship with you because He LOVES you!

I know that may be hard to believe sometimes, and maybe you haven't ever experienced the love of Jesus Christ. And I am a firm believer that you can't feel God's love initially independent of feeling through another human being. That is how He made us.

If you have never been loved, you will not know how to pursue God out of love. You will *embrace his commands* out of guilt, fear, and manipulation. And these motivating factors will spill over into your evangelistic approach. The same thing that motivates you to

God will be the same thing that motivates you to evangelism. Now I am not saying that we do not need a healthy fear (reverence) of God, but it is not my fear of God that motivates me to embrace His commands. Now I must confess that sometimes it is because of consequences. But ultimately I have learned that if it is fear that motivates me, eventually I will give into my flesh and do what I am not supposed to do because eventually my desire to sin is greater than my fear of the consequences of my life. I must learn to do what I do for God because I love Him.

How do I learn to do evangelism out of love for God?

I have to obey His commands. The more I obey, the more I demonstrate my love for God. The more I demonstrate my love for God, the more I am freed by His love to love other human beings. Sin brings fear and death to my life. But obedience over time brings peace, joy, and love. As I see God working in my life, I am amazed by His care and concern for me. If I do not obey Him, I never really see His hand because I am consumed by my lustful selfish desires. I am consumed by them because I refuse to obey, and if I refuse to obey then fear and death are my companions. When fear and death are my companions, I can't feel God's love even though He does love me.

So, obedience doesn't make God love me. It enables me to feel His love. The more obedient I am to His will for my life, the more I am able to focus on His love for me and even feel His love.

Yes, at times embracing God's commands is like meeting a bear in the woods. It isn't easy but it is always a challenge.

God wants to free you from your slavery to sin. He wants to use your life to love others into a real relationship with Jesus Christ. But if you are going to make disobedience the focus of your life, you are never going to feel God's love. If you don't feel God's love, you will feel condemned, and any attempt to reach other people with the Gospel will be condemning, judgmental, and works-oriented. Even the best intentions go awry because human nature gets in the way.

Loving others into a real relationship with Jesus begins with *realizing the cost,* but the only way to maintain a desire to reach the lost as you pay the price is to *embrace his commands.*

What sin do you need to confess to God right now?

What fear are you refusing to place under the Lordship of Christ?

What hidden secret needs to be exposed?

Confess to God your secret.

The best way to re-embrace God's commands is through full disclosure with the Lord.

No secrets.

Confess to God your lack of love for Him because that is what disobedience is. It is us loving sin more than Him. And we all do it. I must confess more than I wish was true.

Ask Him to forgive you.

Ask Him to give you the grace to receive His forgiveness and to appropriate it into your life by asking Him to release you from the condemnation you have felt and are feeling. The Bible tells us that Satan is the Accuser of our lives, not God. Ask God to purge you and cleanse you.

It is not enough just to obey in certain seasons of your life. Listen to what Jesus says...

John 8:31 Jesus said to the people who believed in him, "You are truly my disciples if you keep obeying my teachings. 32 And you will know the truth, and the truth will set you free."

Keep obeying His teaching and over the years you will know the truth (His commands) and the truth will set you free. Free from what?

Free from fear and free to love God like God loves you. Free to love others like God loves you. Free to love others into a real relationship with Jesus Christ.

What sin preoccupies your life? What sin makes you feel temporarily what you want to feel? Do you know the Devil is using that to distract you? Did you know he is using it to put you at ease? He is using it to bring condemnation into your life. He is using it to destroy your love for the lost.

Yeah, it is not easy to fight sin. It is not easy to keep loving God when the temptations seem so great to give into our flesh. Yes, it is a lifetime battle. We know from the Bible that we are never free from this battle. This is true for all of us.

What is the bear in your life?
If you love Him, you will fight to obey Him.
Who do you love more, your sin or God?
Face it.
Let go of your sin.
Love Him.
Keep Embracing His Commands.
How?
I thought you would never ask.
Are you ready to die so you can live?
Are you ready to live so you can love?
Are you ready to embrace Him like you once embraced sin?
Good.
Turn the page.
Let the loving embrace begin.

What's the POINT?

1. What motivates you to do what you do for God?
2. Which commands of Jesus are the most difficult for you to obey?
3. How have you learned to do evangelism for God out of love?

CHAPTER 9

Align Your Allegiance

If any of you wants to be my follower, you must put aside your selfish ambition, shoulder your cross daily, and follow me.

(Luke 9:23)

There it is. The bedrock, the foundation of a real relationship with Jesus Christ. There is nothing glamorous about it. It is not exciting. Matter a fact, it is downright painful to do. It is seemingly humiliating and insignificant at times. But *I have learned over the years that anything of significance generally does not feel significant while it is occurring.* It is usually after the fact looking back that I see that it was important, significant, and life-changing.

If I am going to be in real relationship with Jesus Christ, I have to put aside my selfish ambition. I must die to what I want so God can have what He wants out of my life. I am never free from this battle, and at times it is a beatdown. It is a whole lot easier to throw others under the bus for their sin instead of acknowledging the battle of selfishness that rages inside of me at all turns and at every moment. I am a selfish human being.

Sometimes people say, "I am not a bad person." I say, "I don't think you are a bad person either." But the question is not, "Are you a bad person?" The question is, "Are you a selfless person?" All I can say is, "I am growing." I am learning through my relationship with God, my wife, my kids, my friendships, and my church how to be more selfless with every day.

However, *I hate being selfless.* Do you want to know why? Because selflessness feels like death to me, and death feels futile and depressing to me. I must die to myself so I can live for Him. But I am afraid that if I die to me, living for Him won't feel like life. And so I hold on to my selfishness and live for me because in the moment it feels like life, but ultimately I only eventually feel more death. Why? Because the wages of my selfishness is death. So, if I die to me and choose to live for Him, over time I will feel more alive but less in control. And when I feel less in control, I feel helpless. And when I feel helpless I feel insignificant. And when I feel insignificant, I feel like my life doesn't matter. And when I feel like I don't matter, I sin so I can feel in control again. I become selfish so I can prove to myself and others that I matter. See the vicious cycle of selfishness that leads to sin and death?

Every one of us lives with this battle. Galatians 5:17 says, "The old sinful nature loves to do evil, which is just opposite from what the Holy Spirit wants. And the Spirit gives us desires that are opposite from what the sinful nature desires. These two forces are constantly fighting each other, and your choices are never free from this conflict."

So, what nature are you going to live for, the sinful selfish nature or the Spirit-filled selfless nature? The choice is yours. The choice is mine. We make this decision moment by moment in many areas of our lives.

We can't be godly and live selfish lives. We can't be godly and live self-protective fear-driven lives where we seek to control the outcome and the circumstances of our lives. We must deny ourselves. This is the first step in *aligning our allegiance* to Jesus.

Shoulder your cross daily.... Does that sound exciting? It sounds like a marathon with no water. It sounds like a headache with no aspirin. It sounds like a lot of work and no play. What does it mean to shoulder your cross daily?

If Jesus lived today, do you think he would wear a cross around His neck? Do you think he would think us weird for doing just this? Why do people wear crosses around their neck? The answers to this question could be as great as the amount of people who wear them.

Let me ask the question another way, "Would you wear a gas chamber around your neck?" I know what you're thinking. (He's crazy.) I may be, but it is a legitimate question. See, a gas chamber today symbolizes the same thing a cross did in Jesus' day. The cross symbolized death. It symbolized burdens. It symbolized sacrifice. And because of the resurrection, it symbolized (I believe) life and eternity.

The cross of Jesus symbolized the burdens that He bore for us. Think about it. So why would Jesus tell us to shoulder our crosses daily? Because He wants our lives to symbolize the same thing His did. He wants us to bear the burdens for others. He bore the burdens for us so we could experience eternal life and freedom from sin in this life. And so He wants us to shoulder the cross for others. He wants us to bear burdens for others. You might say, "I need a second opinion."

Look at Galatians 6:2: Share each other's troubles and problems, and in this way obey the law of Christ. 3 If you think you are too important to help someone in need, you are only fooling yourself. You are really a nobody.

Wow, that is pretty clear. He wants us to bear burdens for others and thus fulfill the law of Christ. What is the law of Christ? It is to love God and love people as you love yourself.

So, how often does He want us to bear burdens for others? How often does He want us to shoulder our cross? He said, "daily."

It is easy to do something for a day, a week, a month, a year, maybe even a decade. But God wants us to shoulder our crosses for ourselves and others for a lifetime. It is not how you start but how you finish that matters most.

Are you shouldering your cross daily? Are you bearing burdens for others? Who in your life are you bearing burdens for? Specifically, what "sinner" are you bearing burdens for, so they can come to Christ?

Sharing your faith, you will find out through the progression of this book, is not primarily about a transference of information, but a willingness to bear up under the spiritual burden of carrying someone through religion into a real relationship with Jesus Christ.

Who are you carrying? Write their names down on this page beside this question.

Are you ready for the last part?

Follow Me.

If we knew each other and I said to you, "Follow me," what would you ask me?

I know what I would ask, "Where are we going and what are we going to do?"

Where you go and what you do are not the most important questions to God. They may be to us, but they are not to God. The two most important questions that I believe He wants us to ask are, "How do we live as we go, and who do you want us to become?"

Do you care how you live? Do you care who you are becoming? I don't mean who you are becoming like a lawyer or a daddy or a husband. I mean, like a gentle person, a caring person, a selfless person, a giving person, a loving person. This is what it means to talk about "who" you are becoming. Then the other question is, "How do I live as I go?" How do I give to the people in my life? How do I listen intently and speak gently to this person?

As we progress into the last part of this book, we are going to unpack how I believe God wants us to live among "sinners." I am going to unpack some of the experiences at Vanguard we have had in the process of loving people into a real relationship with Jesus Christ.

Jesus said, "Follow Me."

For my wife and me, that meant we left our homes and went to Liberty University to train for the ministry. It meant we endured a lot of heartaches and challenges in those early years of our relationship. It meant we waited on Him to see what He had for us. It meant after college that we married and moved to Dallas to prepare further for full-time ministry. It meant that after college, we agreed to plant a church with the Southern Baptist Convention in Colorado Springs, CO. It meant years later I would sit in front of a computer and type the ways God broke us from our religious spirit and taught us how to journey in real relationship with Jesus Christ. And you know what it took more than anything else?

Love.
God's love.

But you know what else it took?

A willingness to put aside my selfish ambition, shoulder my cross daily, and follow Him.

I hate dying to self.

I hope one day I hate self more than dying to self.

I am starting to feel alive for others.

I am starting to feel love for others.

Are you willing to *realize the cost*?

It may cost you your religious reputation.

Are you willing to *embrace his commands*?

It requires obedience.

Are you willing to *align your allegiance*?

It is a daily battle.

But Jesus said in Luke 9:24, "If you try to keep your life for yourself, you will lose it. But if you give up your life for me, you will find true life."

Are you tired of living a religious lie? Are you tired of living for you? Are you tired of it being all about you?

Let's lose our religion and multiply Jesus.

Jesus said,

"Vast fields are ripening all around us and are ready now for the harvest. 36 The harvesters are paid good wages, and the fruit they harvest is people brought to eternal life. What joy awaits both the planter and the harvester alike! 37 You know the saying, 'One person plants and someone else harvests.' And it's true. 38 I sent you to harvest where you didn't plant; others had already done the work, and you will gather the harvest."

(John 4:35–38)

Let's get to gathering the harvest of souls for eternity.

What's the POINT?

1. What in your life is not aligned to God's will?
2. What burden is God asking you to bear for other?
3. Where is God asking you to follow Him?

CHAPTER 10

Personally Touch Them

A friend of sinners!

What a title!

This is the name the religious gave to Jesus in His day.

They referred to him as "a friend of sinners." They meant it as an insult. He took it as a compliment.

When people drive by the church you go to, what do they think of your church? Would your church be known as a "friend of sinners?"

Would the religious of your day label you as "a friend of sinners?" Do you have any "friends" in your life who are "sinners"—that is, they don't have a real relationship with Jesus Christ?

I didn't ask, "Do you know lost people?" We all know lost people. I asked, "Do you have anyone in your life who is your friend who is a 'sinner'?"

Jesus did.

Do you?

Remember, WWJD?

He would be a friend to sinners. He would spend time with sinners. He would show love to sinners. He would build relationships with sinners. He would hang out with people who gave him a bad name.

Do you care more about your religious reputation or people? Do you think, "What do the 'religious' people of my life think of my church or what does God think of it?" Do you ever stop to wonder if your church is actually living the Gospel or just preaching the Gospel? Part of teaching the Gospel is living it. It is not what you teach at your church that matters as much as what you live in your life. The world is tired of "Christian preaching." They want to see some "Christian living."

Jesus built relationship with "sinners."

Are you willing to do the same? Are you willing to go where "sinners" are and build relationships with them? Are you willing to lose your religion and pick up the mission of multiplying Jesus' love for others through real relationship?

Good. Then leave your religion here and go with us as we share with you how God changed us and birthed Vanguard Church in Colorado Springs, the Christian mecca of the world, and is teaching us still how to be a friend of sinners in a city where the greatest obstacle to experiencing Jesus is the "religion" of Christianity. In Jesus' day, religion was the biggest obstacle to the Pharisees experiencing Him, and today is no different.

Journey back with me to a time when religion was king and the King of Kings came to change all that.

One day an expert in religious law stood up to test Jesus by asking him this question: "Teacher, what must I do to receive eternal life?"

Jesus replied, "What does the law of Moses say? How do you read it?"

The man answered, " 'You must love the Lord your God with all your heart, all your soul, all your strength, and all your mind.' And, 'Love your neighbor as yourself.'"

"Right!" Jesus told him. "Do this and you will live!"

The man wanted to justify his actions, so he asked Jesus, "And who is my neighbor?"

Luke 10:25–29

Religion meets real relationship.

Religion wants to know "Who is my neighbor?" so we can justify our actions.

Real relationship is looking for someone to love in the name of Jesus.

Religion wants to satisfy the requirements of approval or perceived approval.

Real relationship with Jesus means we are looking for those in need to love.

Why do you do what you do? Do you do it to justify your actions, or do you it because you love God and the people around you? Motivation matters! You can do the same thing in the name of Jesus, but the motive determines the heart, not the action. All actions can be counterfeit of Jesus. The question is not "What should I do for God, but why do I do this?"

God wants us to be motivated to do what we do out of love for Him and love for others.

Do you love the lost? Do you love those outside the church? Are you willing to get dirty to serve others who don't care about the God you love?

I hope the answer is yes. If it is, the question now is "How?"

Where do you start? If relationship matters more to you than religion, then your motivation is love not justification. If love is what matters to you, then you must become a student of other people's lives and ask the question, *"What is the most effective way in our society today to show people the love of Jesus Christ so they have opportunity to experience Him in this life and the life to come?"* Very important question! We believe the most important question.

In modern society, we believe people do not have relationship with God not because they lack the information. The book *Unchristian* revealed in a study in 2008 that 85 percent of sixteen to twenty-nine-year-olds in America know at least five Christians. They said their opinion of Christianity and the church was largely shaped by the relationships they shared with those individuals.

The information that people get about Christianity does not primarily come from the Bible anymore because we are in a post-god, post-church, postmodernity society. Truth is no longer primarily determined through information read in a book, i.e., the Bible. But it is primarily deciphered through relationship. They are decoding God and His Truth through what they experience through you. Scary? It is to me.

But like Christ, we are now the Incarnate representation of the Gospel. However, the difference is He was perfect. We aren't. So eventually we have to bend the knee to the Gospel message and to the "information" that comes through the reality of experiencing Jesus through the Bible. But to start with the Bible in our society is a very ineffective way to begin building relationship with people. Why is this? Because they see the church as hypocritical, judgmental, and because they do not have relationship with you; what you say even if it comes straight from the Bible does not carry huge weight because you have not taken the time to get to know them.

Jesus had an uncanny ability to get to know people and share the truth of who He was and is with them through relationship. He combined modernity and postmodernity in a swift revelation. He could love them, convict them, and teach them at a pace we can't relate to or have the capacity to emulate. But what we can do is learn from him and move at the redeemed but broken pace God has enabled us to move at.

Most of us hate it that we have pain in our lives. We do everything we can to avoid pain. But the longer I live, the more I have discovered that pain is my greatest ally when it comes to being able to relate to humanity in general. I have come to discover that there may only be one universal thing every human being can agree upon and that is, "We all have pain in our lives."

I have never met one person (ever) who has disagreed with me or has said they don't have pain in their lives. It is the universal language that even Jesus understood. It is the path the Father used to redeem us through Jesus, and it is the path God will use to enable us to be used by Jesus Christ to redeem others.

Your pain was uniquely chosen for you so you could be redeemed, and then in turn you could use it to redeem others.

Isaiah 53:5 says, "But he (Jesus) was wounded and crushed for our sins. He was beaten that we might have peace. He was whipped, and we were healed!"

Because of Jesus' pain, we can be healed.

And because of our pain, God will use us through Jesus, to heal others.

No pain in your life is meaningless. Everything you experience is for the sake of redeeming you and redeeming others.

Pain is not a threat to redemption. It is the path.

You can't be redeemed any other way. And you can't be used by God to redeem others any other way.

If we are going to love people into a real relationship with Jesus Christ, we must be willing to initially love them at their greatest points of pain. And oftentimes their pain will be similar to our pain.

So, where do we start? We start at their greatest points of pain. What does this look like?

Do you remember the story of the "Good Samaritan"? Jesus is going to teach us who our neighbor is and the kind of "friend to sinners" he wants us to be.

Jesus said,

"A Jewish man was traveling on a trip from Jerusalem to Jericho, and he was attacked by bandits. They stripped him of his clothes and money, beat him up, and left him half dead beside the road.

"By chance a Jewish priest came along; but when he saw the man lying there, he crossed to the other side of the road and passed him by. A Temple assistant walked over and looked at him lying there, but he also passed by on the other side.

"Then a despised Samaritan came along, and when he saw the man, he felt deep pity. Kneeling beside him, the Samaritan soothed his wounds with medicine and bandaged them. Then he put the man on his own donkey and took him to an inn, where he took care of him. The next day he handed the innkeeper two pieces of silver and told him to take care of the man. 'If his bill runs higher than that,' he said, 'I'll pay the difference the next time I am here.'

"Now which of these three would you say was a neighbor to the man who was attacked by bandits?" Jesus asked.

The man replied, "The one who showed him mercy (love)."

Then Jesus said, "Yes, now go and do the same."

Luke 10:30–37

Maybe you got lost in the story. Maybe you struggle to connect to the donkey, the inn, and the setting surrounding this story. I want to modernize it for you so you can get a greater feeling to what Jesus was conveying.

Once upon a time there was a man who was walking down the road. Two guys got out of the car and beat him up and left him for dead. A senior pastor of a church came along and saw him lying in the ditch on the side of the road. He realized he should help the guy but he was late for church and he knew he had a very important sermon to give that day. So, he rolled down his window and reached across the seat and grabbed an extra Bible, one that was easy to read and relevant for today. He just knew the guy needed a Bible, so He could "get saved." He just knew that if the guy read the Romans road to salvation He would "get saved." So he hurled the Bible out the window and said, "God loves you and has a wonderful plan for your life! Get saved!" The guy rose up out of the ditch wondering who was yelling at him, bloody and battered, and saw a book flying through the air at him. The book hit him square in the head and knocked him out. He fell bloody and battered back into the ditch. He later came to, wondering to himself, *What idiot just hit me in the head with a book?*

A few minutes later, a lay leader of the same church came by. He saw the guy in the ditch but realized he was late for church as well. He was a greeter that day and was responsible for making sure people "feel welcome." He looked at his watch and realized he did have the time to stop and help the guy. In a moment of panic, he felt bad but he also needed to get to church. He noticed a bulletin in the floorboard of the car. He remembered the message from last week being a goodie. So, he reached down in the car and, rolling down the window, he tossed it out the window. As he tossed the bulletin, he yelled, "Come to church, everybody's welcome!" The guy rose up out of the ditch and the bulletin hit him square in the head. It left a paper cut on his forehead. He fell back into the ditch as he thought to himself, *Not again, damn Christians!*

A few minutes later a third person came by. He saw the guy in the ditch. He pulled over to the side of the road, got out, and scooped the guy up in his arms. The man was dirty, bloody, and nasty. He opened the back door of his Hummer 3 (because He was environmentally aware). He put him in the back of his Hummer 3 and drove him to the local hospital. He took the guy into the hospital. Checked him into the hospital and said to the nurse, "Please take care of this guy. Whatever expense He occurs, please put it on my debit card."

And then Jesus says, "Which one was a neighbor to the guy?"

Are you too busy to be in lost people's lives? Is your "good" busy religious schedule keeping you from being in the lives of the lost?

If you are too busy to be in lost people's lives, you are too busy.

How do we lose our religion and multiply Jesus in others?

We personally touch people at their points of pain.

What does it mean to personally touch them? It means you take time out of your good busy religious schedule to look into their eyes and see the hurt of their lives, why they are where they are, and why they do what they do.

Why is this necessary? Because we live in a time known as the INWARD Generation. People are convinced nobody cares about them or what is really going on in their lives. Because of all the postmodern relative truth, their lives do not reflect who they really desire to be. Unfortunately, most look at them and judge them for their external actions as opposed to hearing their heart's cry. Look into their eyes and touch them at their points of pain.

The bottom line is this: you go out of your way to serve them in some capacity in order to show them that you are more concerned about them as people than just about them believing in what some Jesus guy said almost 2000 years ago.

I didn't make this statement up and it is not unique to my generation, but people do not care how much you know until they know how much you care.

When I first met Lillian, I had no idea of the pain she carried in her life. I have since learned that everybody carries heavy pain in their lives in some way or another. Just a brief conversation with her revealed that she had recently lost her mother to cancer. I had recently lost my mom to a drunk driver running over her and killing her.

She wasn't just bearing up under the pain of her mom's death. She was also dealing with having been molested, raped, an abortion, a double mastectomy, and the list goes on and on and on. She had tried to make a deal with the Lord to make her a man. She had given up hope on God and was so confused that she sought to make a deal with the devil. She said in one of the lowest nights of her life, "Satan, if you make me a man, I will give you my soul." She was at the lowest of lows in her life. She saw no hope in her life. I had no idea when I met her for the first time. I had no way of knowing the pain she bore upon her soul and in her life.

The morning God woke my daughter Anastasha up to make cookies for our neighbors, I had no idea that Judy's husband was dying of cancer. God was using Anastasha to bring a personal touch into Judy's life.

When we opened the door to meet Susan, little did we know that she felt lost and unloved in her life and deeply desirous of someone to truly love her.

When I met Steve for the first time, I had no idea that he struggled with alcohol and it was taking control over his life.

Every person I have ever met has pain. The best way for people to initially experience the love of Jesus Christ from you is through you showing compassion, pity, and mercy upon them and what they are going through or have gone through in their lives.

None is by accident, and you will discover over and over again that God was preparing you all along to meet certain people in your life and help them as you yourself have been helped. Paul talks about this in Corinthians.

"He (God) comforts us in all our troubles so that we can comfort others.

1 Corinthians 1:4

For years I resented God for allowing my mother to be killed by a drunk driver. Now over two decades later I accept that my mother's death has been used over and over again not only to bring comfort to so many people of faith, but also to help bring others to faith.

When the world feels that we understand their pain, they are more inclined to trust us.

Trust is the beginning of a real relationship between you, the unbeliever, and God.

Trust with an unbeliever is established initially through *touching* them with the Gospel, not initially *telling* them about the Gospel.

You must establish credibility with the unbeliever through shared experiences, not initially through your knowledge of Scripture or your awareness of their destiny. They must discover their lostness through your compassion. You must help them discover it through being willing to let them see the pain in your life that has created chaos and confusion. They must be allowed to feel the comfort you have received from Christ through the pain you have faced. This comfort may very well be the greatest evidence of God in your life, especially the comfort you pass on to them that Christ has given you through your faith in Him.

Do you know anybody in your life who needs a personal touch? Are you a busy religious person? Do want to be the best disciple of Jesus Christ you can possibly be? Good; begin to befriend "sinners" at their greatest points of pain. Show them compassion. Bother yourself with their needs.

If you want to be a real disciple of Christ, you must be a neighbor like the Good Samaritan.

Personally touch them ... careful, though ... you won't ever be the same again.

When you feel someone else's pain, the compassion of Jesus will be released in your heart, and then you will discover like never before....

It ain't all about you anymore. I am here to be a "friend of sinners."

Beware, though, the religious will be there to say, "You're bringing Satan into this church with your friendships. You are a friend of those 'sinners.'"

They mean it as an insult, but you just look at them and say, "Thanks. I take it as a compliment. Because I am most like Jesus when I am personally touching the 'sinners' of the world."

What's the POINT?

1. Would the religious of your day label you a "friend of sinners"?
2. What religious spirit do you need to give up?
3. What points of pain in your life could God use to redeem others?

CHAPTER 11

Occassionally Encourage Them

Once you start caring for a person at their greatest points of pain, you must be willing to back off and give them a chance to process the comfort they have experienced from you.

Most people don't like being indebted to others, especially in areas of care. It makes us feel vulnerable to know we have shared some of the deepest places of our hearts. It is uncomfortable to know that someone has had a "power" of sorts over our lives, and unbelieving people are no different.

It is hard for them to imagine that they have let you into their life. They are still raw and confused by the experiences of their lives and often they may distance themselves from you, maybe not physically or even emotionally, but spiritually.

You must understand that once you have touched an unbeliever at one of their greatest points of pain and they feel the comfort of God that flows through you, it triggers a spiritual battle inside of them that even they may not be aware of is taking place. They feel things that are oftentimes seemingly strange and out of control.

They may feel indebted to you and may expect that you have something you want from them. Or they may not feel the pain they felt anymore and thus they don't need or want you in their lives at that level anymore. This is where you must be patient. Like any relationship, it does not develop in a day and it won't completely change in a day. You must be patient. You must be committed at this point to praying for them. You must also, because of the needs and responsibilities of your life, continue with all the other relationships and responsibilities that are entrusted to you. Just like you can't rest, sleep, work out, vacation, or relax all the time, you can't just sit around and do nothing until they want to meet again. You must be willing to back off if they need it. But in the midst of backing off, you must also look for opportunities to engage them.

So then what do you do? You look for opportunities to occasionally encourage them.

What does it look like to occasionally encourage them?

Jesus was a master at this.

One thing that Jesus often did was make religious people mad. As a matter a fact, the only time he ever got mad was when he went to church. One way He most often made religious people mad was by eating with what the religious people called "sinners." Jesus loved to eat with "sinners."

Luke illustrates this in one of his stories...

"Soon Levi held a banquet in his home with Jesus as the guest of honor. Many of Levi's fellow tax collectors and other guests were there. But the Pharisees (the religious) and their teachers of religious law complained bitterly to Jesus' disciples, "Why do you eat and drink with such scum?"

Jesus answered them, "Healthy people don't need a doctor—sick people do. I have come to call sinners to turn from their sins, not to spend my time with those who think they are already good enough.

Luke 5:29–32

Who do you spend your time with? Do you see yourself as sick? Have you ever looked at someone and said, "That person is sick." Or have you ever said to someone, "You make me sick."

Jesus said, "He came to spend time with the sick." He came to show compassion to those who were in need of a healing in their lives. Pain leaves us needing a healing in our lives one way or another. Compassion and time spent with the unbeliever is how we show them an occasional encouragement.

A number of years ago my family went away on a family vacation. Every other year we go on a "big trip." We had just given birth to our third child, Joshua, and we desperately wanted to get away from ministry for a while, unwind, regroup, and reconnect with each other.

We left for the Northwest and were en route to Oregon. Through a series of events, we ended up in Seattle, Washington (a place we had never been). We found a hotel and settled in for a few days. I went down to the hotel lobby to a coffee shop called Tully's near downtown Seattle and sought to spend some "quality" time with God.

Ah, finally, some alone time from the kids; with Bible and journal in hand, I just knew this was going to be a great time.

I found a corner table looking out the window at one of the downtown streets of Seattle. Everyone was hustling back in forth with latte in hand. It was Seattle's Best. If you are a coffee drinker, you know what I mean.

After a few minutes of being in the coffee shop and journaling, for some reason I looked up. I noticed a street person coming toward the coffee shop. For whatever reason, I felt burdened for this man. I had never seen him before in my life and didn't care honestly if I ever did see him again. I was here to relax not do ministry.

I felt the mercy of God swell in my heart for this man. I hated it.

I felt like the Lord said, *I want you to show "encouragement" to this man. What?* I said to myself in my head.

God, I am here to vacation not do ministry.
Remember the Good Samaritan. Maybe he was on vacation as well; maybe he was in a hurry to get to his vacation destination.

Oh, how I wanted to push these sorts of thoughts out of my head. It made me angry.

God, I have given you my life, can't I just have a moment of silence? Can't I be left alone for just a little while? I have come all these miles to relax and recover from ministry and you want me to do more ministry?

Honestly, at that moment I didn't care about that man's eternity. I didn't care that he was in the ditch. I didn't care how he got there and I didn't care to help him, at all!

As I look at this man, I got the impression in my head, *Buy this man a latte!*

What? Buy a homeless crippled man a $4 coffee drink? Now, isn't that the most ridiculous thing you have ever heard in your life?

I drifted back into Bible reading like any good Christian pastor would do. My religion was to read the Bible, not live it.

Ouch!

The next thing I remember was hearing the ding of the doorbell as someone opened the door to the coffee shop. I looked and, to my amazement, the homeless crippled man was coming into the shop with his shopping cart.

I just shook my head and thought, *What in the world is a homeless crippled man with a shopping cart doing coming into a nice coffee shop?*

I judged him greatly.

He has no business in here, I thought to myself.

He made his way to the counter to order a drink. I felt the Lord say to me again, *Go buy him a coffee drink!*

I said to the Lord, *Right, I am going to go buy a homeless crippled man a specialty coffee.*

The Lord said, *That's right. Now stand up and go do it!*

I don't know how you know when Jesus is speaking to you, but I have known since I was a little boy that when Jesus is speaking to me, my heart starts racing really fast. I get extremely scared and I feel an amazing battle of the will being unleashed in my heart.

The homeless man limped over to the counter.

Everything was getting louder in my head.

My heart kept racing.

I felt God screaming to me, *Get up!*

I stood.

It was like an out-of-body experience. I could see myself.

I could hear the voices, *You're an idiot. What is wrong with you? He is going to think you are crazy. What are all these people going to think?*

I walked up behind him.

He ordered his $4 coffee. The girl behind the counter rang up his drink and said, "That will be...."

He started to pay ... I opened my mouth ... and out came ... "I will buy it."

He turned around and just glared at me. He said nothing at all.

It was awkward at best.

He stunk and I was scared.

Two strangers thrown together in a coffeehouse ditch on the side of Seattle's Best.... How many people passed this guy and left him coffeeless?

Big deal, I bought the guy coffee.

Big deal? Buying this guy coffee would prove to change my life and reveal to me the deep heart of the Father for those found on the side of life's road.

I paid and returned to my seat.

He grabbed a newspaper and sat down at a table near my table.

I returned to my seat and sat down. My back was to him.

The thought occurred to me, *He didn't say, "Thanks."* Ungrateful homeless dude!

I started getting angry that he didn't thank me.

Then I said to the Lord, *Okay, Lord, what do I do now?*

I felt like the Lord said, *Nothing.*

Nothing, what do you mean nothing? I thought to myself.

I drove over a thousand miles to a coffee shop near downtown Seattle and bought a homeless crippled dude coffee and now I am to do nothing?

I felt like the Lord said, *That's right.*

Confusion flooded over me. *Why, Lord?*

I felt like the Lord said, *Because that is what I do and I wanted you to be like me. I give good gifts to people with no strings attached.*

As simple as this moment was, it was profound.

Can I do something for someone with nothing in return even if I don't get thanked?

An occasional encouragement is when you use the resources that have been entrusted to you by God to serve others expecting nothing in return. Can you use your house to invite people over for dinner and not expect anything in return? Can you buy a homeless dude a $4 coffee and live with him not saying thank you and not thinking that you are supposed to "get him saved?"

Can you cut your neighbor's lawn without them even knowing it? Can you make cookies and take them to your neighbors and leave them on their doorstep with a note saying, "Just because you're my neighbor."

Can you occasionally encourage the lost without expecting anything in return or being repaid for your eternal kindness?

Jesus said...

"When you put on a luncheon or a dinner," he said, "don't invite your friends, brothers, relatives, and rich neighbors. For they will repay you by inviting you back. Instead, invite the poor, *the crippled,* the lame, and the blind. Then at the resurrection of the godly, God will reward you for inviting those who could not repay you."

Luke 14:12–14

Who does God want you to occasionally encourage? Who does He want you to use your resources and life to serve, expecting nothing in return?

I want to challenge you to go into a coffee shop and sit down in a corner and say to the Lord, "God, show me who you want me to buy a coffee for today." Then when He reveals it to you, get up, go buy the coffee. Pay for it. Go back, sit down, and return to your business. If they ask, "Why did you do this?" Say, "Because that is what Jesus does for me. He gives me things expecting nothing in return."

Remember Lillian? The woman I thought was a man? The one I invited to our home for dinner and to be a part of our spiritual discussion group in our home?

He wanted to invite his friend Jennifer, who I assumed was his girlfriend.

Well, as you remember, he was a she. And Jennifer turned out to be her lesbian lover.

What? I invited a lesbian couple to my home?

I grew up on a dairy farm in Kentucky. I don't know anything about lesbian lovers.

What if while we are having dinner she leans across to her lesbian lover and kisses her?

What do I do then?

My anxiety level went through the roof.

I want to use my home to minister to people but come on, God, you have to give me a little help here!

Do you know what? Lillian and Jennifer were a delight to have for dinner.

Whether it is a homeless dude needing a coffee from a selfish guy like me or a lesbian couple needing a meal in the home of a judgmental pastor like me, the occasional encouragements that I have given to people have impacted me probably more than they have impacted those who were recipients of my kindness.

Trust me. It changed my life.

Trust me. It will change your life.

Trust Him. It will change their lives.

Do something for someone you know or someone you don't and expect nothing in return.

Get outside your selfishness and judgmental spirit and use your resources to ... occasionally encourage others. It will go a long way in helping you take risks to reach the lost.

What's the POINT?

1. Who do you see as sick?
2. How are you reading religion but not living it?
3. What good gifts can you give others?

CHAPTER 12

Interactively Listen to Them

I believe the Bible is full of errors.
I don't think it is a sin to be homosexual.
I think it is okay to get a sex change.
I don't believe Jesus is the only way to eternal life.
I don't believe Jesus is God.
I don't believe in God.
I gave my soul to Satan.

These are just a few of the statements I have heard over the years while seeking to love people into a REAL relationship with Jesus Christ.

What would you say to someone if they said, "I don't think it is a sin to be homosexual"?

How would you respond? How have you responded in the past?

Just a few weeks into our new little Vanguard church plant, Lillian said to me, "I don't think homosexuality is a sin."

I listened. And what I have learned is that if you listen to people who make controversial statements, eventually they will ask you what you think if they respect and trust you.

So, I listened to Lillian's life.

One time, Lillian came over to the house and sat at our dining room table and told Tosha (my wife) and me, "I want to get a sex change. I want to become a man."

What would you do with that?

We listened.

One time, Steve came over to the house and we sat and talked. He said, "I believe the Bible is full of errors."

What would you do with that?

We listened.

One time, Susan shared, "I don't believe Jesus claimed to be God. I believe that is something that Christians made up."

What would you do?

We listened.

One time, Denise shared, "I don't believe Jesus is God."

What would you do?

We listened.

One time, John shared, "I believe if there is an eternal life, Jesus is just a way to eternal life but not the only way."

What would you do?

We listened.

Why?

As Christians always say, "WWJD," what would Jesus do?

I am glad you asked.

John 4 records the story of Jesus and the Samaritan woman.

It is classic Jesus. For sake of time, I will tell the story and summarize the events to get to the point. Jesus had been baptizing and making lots of disciples. The Pharisees were trying to divide him and John by saying, "Jesus has more disciples than John." Jesus got wind of this, left Judea, and returned to Galilee.

Usually when a Jew left Judea and went to Galilee, they would go the long way around instead of taking the shortcut through Samaria. Samaritans were half-Jewish and half-Gentiles. The Jews considered them "unclean dogs." So the Jews avoided them at all cost similar to how Christians today in America have a tendency to avoid the poor, the homosexual, and a people with AIDS.

Jesus, on the other hand, looked for opportunities to be in the presence of despicable people. He wanted to be around people the religious community shunned. So he went straight through Samaria. On the way he came to Jacob's well and sat down beside it about noontime.

Eventually a Samaritan woman came to draw water. I have been taught since my childhood that no one in their right mind gathered water at noon, during the hottest part of the day, unless that person was trying to avoid others. I have always been taught that this woman was probably trying to avoid the other women. She had a "reputation," if you know what I mean. You know anyone like that?

She came to the well to draw water.

Jesus was there.

Since Jesus is God, one can assume that Jesus knew what kind of woman she was. Maybe He had even orchestrated these events. Maybe this was a divine moment. I tend to think it was.

He already knew everything about this woman. We eventually learn this later in the story. He already knew her reputation, her past. She was a "woman" with a reputation. She had had five husbands, and the man she was living with at present was not her husband.

She was a slut. (Okay I said it, but you were thinking it!)

Everybody knew her name, at least the men of the town.

If you were Jesus and this woman showed up at the well, just you and her, what would you say to her?

Would you look her in the eye and say, "Hey, slut, when do you plan on cleaning up your life and living a godly life, one similar to whom God created you to originally be?"

Would you say, "You disgust me, you despicable person!"

Would you say, "You're going to hell, whore!"

Do you know what Jesus said? He said, "Please, give me a drink." He asked her a question. He asked her for something. Why do you think Jesus asked her a question?

After Jesus asked the question, the Bible says,

John 4:9: The woman was surprised, for Jews refuse to have anything to do with Samaritans. She said to Jesus, "You are a Jew, and I am a Samaritan woman. Why are you asking me for a drink?"

She was surprised.

He crossed racial barriers, gender barriers, and religious barriers to ask her a question.

Why?

Because when you ask someone a question, you bring dignity to their life. When you ask someone who knows they need your help to help you, it brings respect and love to their soul.

Jesus brought dignity to this woman's life by asking her a question and listening. He could have destroyed her with his knowledge of her immorality. He could have led with what He knew about her. He could have said, "Repent, you whore!" He could have called her a slut and it would have been accurate. She was not a good woman. She was not a pure and godly woman. She was living a duplicitous life. He knew it. She knew it.

But what did he do?

He asked her a question and then he listened.

This is called *interactively listening.*

You ask a question and then you listen.

Jesus was a master at this.

Yes, he eventually got to the big questions, but he didn't start with them. He led with questions instead of comments. When someone says something to you that you don't agree with, do you respond with a statement or a question?

A statement means you don't agree and you are going to judge them for it. A question means you want to understand why they believe the way they do before you share your view on what they believe.

This is a drastic shift from being driven with comments and information to being driven by questions and a desire to listen. When we ask questions and listen, we convey to people our care for them. It shows that their opinion matters to us and it brings dignity, respect, and love to their lives.

I have learned over the years that people do not know why they believe what they do, they just know what they believe and then they live accordingly. I want to challenge you to change the way you approach this and take a more interactive approach. Instead of combating how people live or even what they say they believe, always lead with the question, "Why do you believe that?" More often than not I hear people say, "I don't know." Then after they pause for a while, they say, "There was this guy...," and they begin to tell me this story about someone in their life that hurt them. Or, "I don't understand why God would..." and then they begin to tell me a story about how they feel abandoned and hurt by God.

I have learned that people primarily believe what they do because of what they have experienced through relationship with God and others. And pain is the primary motivator that has shaped their faith view or lack thereof.

Do you need a second opinion?

John 8 - Oh, I know it is not supposed to be in the Bible, but it is.

The woman caught in the very act of adultery. Can you imagine?

The Bible says that while Jesus was teaching, the teachers of religious law and Pharisees brought a woman they had caught in the very act of adultery. Not sure what happened to the guy in the equation.

They put her in front of the crowd.

They wanted Jesus to judge her.

The Bible tells us that Jesus knelt down and wrote in the dirt. Why do you think he did this?

I have been told various reasons, we don't know for sure. So, here we go: I want to tell you my version of why I think Jesus wrote in the dirt.

The Bible says the Pharisees said, "This woman was caught in the *very* act of adultery."

Can you imagine? They went in the bedroom and there they were.

Wonder who the man was? Wonder where the man went? Did they set her up?

We don't know. Anyway, here is my question: "Do you commit the very act of adultery with or without your clothes on?"

I am going to say the odds are she was naked.

Do you think the religious walked in and said, "Stop doing that—get dressed, we are going to go see Jesus"?

Maybe, but I doubt it.

If they caught her in the very act of adultery it is my estimation that they brought her as they found her—naked.

I believe the woman stood before God (Jesus) and everybody naked. I believe Jesus knelt down and wrote in the dirt to show respect to this naked woman. I believe He was trying to restore her dignity in the midst of the religious spirit that surrounded both of them.

She was in the wrong, no doubt. But so were they. And Jesus didn't want to have anything to do with using religion to destroy people for the wrong they have done. He came to save, not judge.

Eventually he said, "He who is without sin, cast the first stone." Well, the church service caught quiet and before long everybody went home.

They got it.

What was the first thing Jesus said to this woman?

The first thing he said was, "Where are your accusers?"

He got rid of the religious before he ever addressed the "sinner." Interesting, isn't it?

He asked her a question. Why? Because questions bring dignity to people's lives and give them a chance to learn and experience God. I find that God most convicts me with questions, not statements, and He did the same for this woman in her situation.

Then He followed it up with another question, "Didn't even one of them condemn you?"

She answers, "No, Lord," she said.

She already understands more about Him as Lord than they have in years.

Finally Jesus said to her, "Neither do I. Go and sin no more."

He is not okay with us living sinful lives, but sin is not the primary focus of God, it is the sinner.

I challenge you to read through the Gospels; you will begin to notice that this is the approach Jesus takes. He asks questions and then he listens.

This is what He began to teach me when we came to start Vanguard in 1996.

One time Lillian said to me, "Kelly, what do you think about my homosexuality?"

And, for whatever reason, and I believe it was God. I felt like the Lord said, *Kelly, say to her, "I didn't create you. I didn't die for you. I won't be your judge. So it doesn't matter what I think about your homosexuality."*

So, I said it just like that.

She was stunned, and so was I.

My religious fear came over me. I thought, *What if she thinks I approve of her lifestyle?* Oh, no, my opinion is so important to this universe. What if she thinks I think homosexuality is okay? Fear swelled inside of me.

Don't we have a responsibility to tell the world that it is living in sin?

Let's see what the Bible has to say about that question...

1 Corinthians 5:9,

"When I wrote to you before, I told you not to associate with people who indulge in sexual sin. 10 But I wasn't talking about unbelievers who indulge in sexual sin, or who are greedy or are swindlers or idol worshipers. You would have to leave this world to avoid people like that. 11 What I meant was that you are not to associate with anyone who claims to be a Christian yet indulges in sexual sin, or is greedy, or worships idols, or is abusive, or a drunkard, or a swindler. Don't even eat with such people.

12 *It isn't my responsibility to judge outsiders,* but it certainly is your job to judge those inside the church who are sinning in these ways. 13 *God will judge those on the outside."*

Did you catch that? It is not our job to judge those on the outside."of the church who are in sin. Matter a fact, if we do, it is us that is in sin. That is right. If the church is preoccupied with judging the world, we are in sin ourselves. It is not our job to judge the world. Jesus didn't come to condemn but to save it.

(John 3:17)

So if Jesus didn't come to condemn the world, then why are we? These are the things God was teaching me.

I was fighting a battle inside myself to want to control the situation and tell her the "truth" and listen to God and do what He tells me to do. I yielded and listened.

I then heard the Lord say to me, *Have her ask me what I think about her homosexuality.*

So, in my head I prayed this prayer, "Lord, have her ask me what You think about her homosexuality."

About two months past and we were preparing for our first outreach event as a new church plant. She was helping us get ready and she turned to me and said, "Kelly, what does God think about my homosexuality?"

I turned away immediately, tearing up. I couldn't believe God had answered my prayer. I know, I know. I am a Christian but not a very good one.

I turned back to her and said, "Do you have a Bible?"

She said, "No."

I told her I would get her a Bible and mark Romans 2 and 1 Corinthians 6. She could read them and then we would get together and discuss it.

She did.

We got together again and I asked her, "What does the Bible have to say about homosexuality?"

She said, "It says it is a sin."

I was floored. Can you believe that? The Bible has the power to change lives. I thought it was my opinion of the Bible. I thought it was my ability to explain the Bible. I thought it was ME. No, I am just the conduit called to love people; *it is the Bible that changes people, not us.*

A few weeks later she gave her heart to Jesus Christ.

About six months later Lillian, my wife Tosha, and I stood before 15,000 Southern Baptist in Ft. Worth, Texas, and she shared this story with them.

It was amazing!

Interactively listen.

Ask questions.

Listen.

Ask questions.

Listen.

Ask questions.

Listen.

After hearing Lillian's story, I wouldn't have wanted to be gay or get a sex change. I would have probably already killed myself. She had endured all manner of evil in her life. She had been molested, raped, and abused.

I often say, "If you don't know a sinner, it is easy to tell them the 'truth.' It is easy to judge them. But if you know a sinner, it is hard to tell them the truth because you begin to see the 'why' of why they are where they are."

This doesn't mean that they don't have to take responsibility for their story. What it means is that their story is what helps you to understand them. And when you understand why they do what they do instead of what, it enables you to see, empathize, and have compassion for the brokenness of their lives.

God changed me that day. I have never been the same since.

I have learned.

Ask questions.

Listen.

Ask the Lord to have them ask you questions about Him.

When they want to know what He thinks.

Then share the Word of God with them.

Let them read it.

Ask them what it says.

Listen.

If God is drawing them and they are listening to Him through His Word, they will mirror back to you what He thinks about their lives and their sin.

Listen.

It changed my life and eventually theirs.

It can change yours, too.

Are you listening?

What's the POINT?

1. How do you respond when an unbeliever asks you what you think of their lifestyle?
2. What religious fear do you need to put to death?
3. How can you learn to be a better listener and question asker?

CHAPTER 13

Never Give Up on Them

Never give up on them....

Are you tired? Are you discouraged? Do you feel like giving up? Did you think God was doing something through this relationship you have developed and now you are wondering?

Maybe it was just in your head?

You call.

They don't return your call.

You email.

They don't email you back.

You stop by their house and ring the doorbell.

They don't come to the door.

You wait, wait, and then wait some more.

What do you do?

Never give up on them but give them space.

In Luke 15:4 Jesus tells us a story:

"If you had one hundred sheep, and one of them strayed away and was lost in the wilderness, wouldn't you leave the ninety-nine others to go and search for the lost one until you found it?

8 Or suppose a woman has ten valuable silver coins and loses one. Won't she light a lamp and look in every corner of the house and sweep every nook and cranny until she finds it? 9 And when she finds it, she will call in her friends and neighbors to *rejoice with her because she has found her lost coin.* 10 In the same way, there is joy in the presence of God's angels when even one sinner repents."

These are beautiful illustrations of how God never gives up on us. But what if they give up on us? What if they leave us? What if they take the goods we have taught them, given them, and shared with them and leave?

What do you do then?

I am glad you asked. Jesus addresses this as well in the illustration of the Lost Son in Luke 15:11 …

"**11** To illustrate the point further, Jesus told them this story: "A man had two sons. 12 The younger son told his father, '*I want my share of your estate now, instead of waiting until you die.*' So his father agreed to divide his wealth between his sons.

13 A few days later this younger son packed all his belongings and took a trip to a distant land, and *there he wasted all his money on wild living.*

14 *About the time his money ran out, a great famine swept over the land,* and he began to starve.

15 He persuaded a local farmer to hire him to feed his pigs.
16 The boy became so hungry that even the pods he was feeding the pigs looked good to him. *But no one gave him anything."*

Why do you think no one gave him anything? This is just conjecturing, but possibly because God didn't want him to have anything. Everything we have comes from God. His father gave him his inheritance, but ultimately it came from God.

Why would God not want this man to have anything? Because He wanted to get his attention so he would come back to his father.

It is important to realize that when an unbeliever abandons you, don't see it as a rejection of you. See it as a rejection of the Gospel. See it as conviction upon their lives. See it as,

"They are just not ready, yet."

Never give up on them but give them their space.

I don't call this my stray sheep theology, lost coin theology, or lost son theology, but my stray dog theology. Why? Well, first of all, I don't know. Then second of all, I came up with my own illustration from my childhood that resonated with me and I think it might with you as well.

Personally I didn't have any lost sheep growing up, but I did have a lot of lost dogs and stray dogs. Growing up on a dairy farm, we often had stray dogs come around for food.

Just like the lost son, they had left something. I didn't know their history just as I don't know the lost person's history. They just magically appear one day on the doorstep of our milk barn looking for something to eat, similar to how the lost son showed up at the local farmer looking to him to hire him to feed his pigs.

He was hungry. They are hungry. I have found over the years that lost people don't necessarily know they are spiritually hungry for God when they show up in my life or when our paths cross on the basketball court or at a coffee shop. But I have learned that regardless of whether they realize they are hungry for God, everyone knows they are hungry for something even if they don't know that the something is a someone.

What is the first thing you learn about a stray dog?

They are scared of you most of the time.

Do you know the first thing I usually always learn about unbelievers?

They are scared of me if they know I am Christian.

They are afraid I am going to convert them. They are afraid I am going to try to make them something they don't want to be. But mostly they are afraid I am going to judge them and condemn them like many other Christians in their lives have done to them in the past.

The book *Unchristian* says the top two reasons why people don't want anything to do with church is because of hypocrisy and our judgmental spirit toward them.

The last thing a stray dog wants is to be kicked around by a stranger.

Their life is hard enough. Their existence is difficult enough.

The last thing an unbeliever wants is to be kicked around and judged for the past they have lived. Their life has been hard enough. They know deep down they are condemned. They feel it. They live it every day. They feel the consequence of their sin. They feel the deep dark brokenness of their lives that they can hide from maybe everyone but themselves.

They are lost.

They are stray.

They are hungry spiritually whether they know it or not, but **they are more afraid of being hurt again than getting help.** Can you relate in your life? I can.

Why is this? Because they do not trust you. They don't know you. They are not sure you have their best interest in mind.

A stray dog is the same.

If I were to put food and water beside the stray dog to get fresh water and food, and let's assume he has not eaten in days, do you think he would come up to the bowl while I am standing beside it?

More than likely, NOT!

Why? He is afraid of me.

Do you think the average unbeliever in our post-god society is going to be okay with us walking up to them cold turkey and saying to them, "Get saved or you are going to hell!"

Statistics show in *Unchristian* that the greatest damage you can do to an unbeliever is to tell them something like this when you don't know them or have taken the time to get to know them.

Luke 15:1 says...

"Tax collectors and other notorious sinners often came to listen to Jesus teach. 2 This made the Pharisees and teachers of religious law complain that he was associating with such despicable people—even eating with them."

Did you catch that? *Tax collectors and other notorious sinners often came to listen to Jesus teach.*

Jesus was not a cold turkey evangelist contrary to what we may have been taught or have chosen to believe. Yes, there are times he called people out immediately, but it was to *heal* them, not *tell* them something about their eternity.

I can't find anywhere in the Bible where someone was not being pursued or previously moved by the Spirit to experience God that someone in the Bible came up to them and, on the spot, just "got 'em saved."

Relationship is king.
And the story of their life is the way to their heart.

95

Until you build trust, they are not going to eat out of your bowl of wisdom regarding God, Jesus, and salvation.

Someone once said, "They don't care how much you know until they know how much you care."

Earn the right to speak into their lives. We do this through personal touch, occasional encouragement, interactively listening to them, and choosing never to give up on them, but giving them their space.

Put the food in the bowl of their soul and move away. Let them experience something from you with no strings attached and no pressing requests from you. Give them space. Serve them and back away.

Give God time to create the circumstances in their lives that enable you to care for them again. Everyone has needs, eventually.

But know this: once you put the food in the bowl, back away and wait.

The stray dog comes to the bowl, eats the food, and then goes over next to you and lies down. Right?

No, he eats the food, looks around, licks his chops, and then ...

... *he runs off.*

Unbelievers are the same way. You serve them. You love them. You listen to them.

Then when their hunger is gone, so are they.

It is the hunger that is bringing them to you. It is God's Spirit through you that is feeding them. But no one can keep eating. And it takes maturity and faith to realize that the food is what changed and satisfied them. Once they are satisfied, they are gone.

Be patient. Give them their space. Back away and don't be so insecure that you get wrapped up into the rejection you just experienced.

I can remember when we first started Vanguard we hosted a group for unbelievers, and two weeks in a row nobody came.

I remember sitting down in my chair and thinking to myself, *I can't do this anymore. I just can't take the failure and the rejection.* I wanted to quit. I started to scheme on how I could say, "This is not God's will."

My devotions that day were John 10:11,

"I am the good shepherd. The good shepherd lays down his life for the sheep. 12 A hired hand will run when he sees a wolf coming. He will leave the sheep because they aren't his and he isn't their shepherd. And so the wolf attacks them and scatters the flock. 13 The hired hand runs away because he is merely hired and has no real concern for the sheep."

I heard the Lord say that day, *Which kind of shepherd are you going to be to my sheep?*

It broke me. I committed myself that day to ministry and to reaching the lost in Colorado Springs.

I got up and recommitted myself.

Thousands got saved the next day.

Right?

No!

Not much changed. Matter of fact, nobody came the next week either.

Stray dogs are hard to catch and even harder to tame.

But rest assured when they get hungry they know where to go. They come back to where they know they can eat. It just takes them time to realize they are hungry and tired of what the world has to offer.

And there you are, once again putting food in the bowl, backing away and letting the stray eat.

Eventually, you know what will happen to the strays that keep coming back to you? They will let you get closer to them.

They will eventually let you touch them, hold them, bathe them, love them, and become your friend. That's right, over time you become "a friend of sinners" just like Jesus.

You have to fight through the insecurity, the demonic attacks, the feeling of rejection and failure, and be patient. You must never give up on them but give them their space. It is in God's timing not yours.

They are His sheep, and when He calls they hear His voice.

Your voice is only powerful in their life if you are allowing Him to speak through you.

You wake up one morning and just like the father who lost his son, look what happens ...

"When he finally came to his senses, he said to himself, 'At home even the hired men have food enough to spare, and here I am, dying of hunger! 18 I will go home to my father and say, "Father, I have sinned against both heaven and you, 19 and I am no longer worthy of being called your son. Please take me on as a hired man."'

20 So he returned home to his father. And while he was still a long distance away, his father saw him coming. *Filled with love and compassion, he ran to his son, embraced him, and kissed him. 21 His son said to him, 'Father, I have sinned against both heaven and you, and I am no longer worthy of being called your son.'*

22 But his father said to the servants, 'Quick! Bring the finest robe in the house and put it on him. Get a ring for his finger, and sandals for his feet. 23 And kill the calf we have been fattening in the pen. We must celebrate with a feast, 24 for this son of mine was dead and has now returned to

life. He was lost, but now returned to life. He was lost, but now he is found.' So the party began.

So the party began."

Luke 15:17

Steve (the guy who helped move our couch in) came to Christ five years after we met on that first night we moved to Colorado Springs. What little did we know that night would be a night that would begin a five-year "stray dog" relationship. He experienced the death of one of his close friends and a potentially terminal illness in his immediate family.

On our fifth anniversary as a church, Steve shared with the entire church that he had begun a real relationship with Jesus Christ.

Steve and his family moved shortly after that to North Carolina. A few years later we went to see them. We were at their house for dinner and Steve said, "Let's pray." He prayed the best prayer I have ever heard. It brought tears to my eyes. He and I continue to stay in touch from time to time.

Lillian gave her life to Jesus Christ along with her partner. Lillian eventually moved away. We tried to stay in touch but lost touch over time. I haven't talked to her in years. The last time I talked with her she was doing okay, not great. It breaks my heart to think of the pain that poor girl carries in her heart.

Lillian's partner, Jennifer, left Colorado Springs and went to Japan to teach English as a second language. She came back a year later for a few weeks and shared with us that God had been using her to share Christ with a Buddhist priest in Japan. Wow, how the Gospel travels. It travels best in the hearts of people changed by it. She eventually landed in Oklahoma.

Susan married, divorced, and eventually moved away from our community of faith without having ever begun a real relationship with Jesus Christ. She landed in the Dallas Fort Worth area. We lost touch with her.

One day she called to say, "I gave my life to Jesus Christ." I was blown away. Here is this stargazer now walking with Jesus Christ. I was jealous, though, because we had done all the "hard work" and someone else got to reap the benefit. Yes, it shows my immaturity and selfishness in the kingdom of God.

Susan came back to see us one time. Tosha asked her if she remembered the first conversation we had with her and the follow-up conversation. She said, "Vaguely." Tosha refreshed her memory by telling her how we encouraged her to read the Gospel of John and she came back and said, "I read what you told me to and then I read Matthew, Mark, and Luke, as well and you know what I realized? It's the same damn story."

She still playfully denies it to this day. But we still laugh about her honest response to the synoptic gospels. I love lost people. I love their realness. I love the fact that they have no religious pretense.

Denise gave her heart to Jesus but soon after left our church and joined another one where she could attend with her mother. It was very difficult to say goodbye to someone we had worked so hard to bring into the kingdom. I wish I could say my first thought is to be kingdom minded, but I am more prone to be selfish minded.

She came back to our church again years later and even worked for a local Christian organization in our city. We have great respect and appreciation for her and she for us, but for whatever reason after she came to Christ, our church just wasn't a fit for her. This is hard to make sense of, but I must keep in mind that we are to be about the work of God, not the work of building our own kingdom here on earth.

And yes, there were those who we never got a chance to reach with the love of Jesus Christ.

We moved from our neighborhood where Judy lived, and though we promised ourselves we would not lose touch with her, we did. Even the best of good intentions sometimes go awry.

And I could tell you story after story of people who eventually rejected us and wouldn't return our calls, our emails, or respond to our attempts to never give up on them but give them their space. Sometimes the space becomes so great that you have to let them go, but I still hope above hope that God will bring them back like the lost son came back to his father.

Just this past week in our worship services, a woman came up to me and said, "Do you remember me?" I said, "Your face looks familiar, but I don't remember your name." She told me her name and said, "Eleven years ago you invited me to church and here we are."

Eleven years later. Wow!

Don't give up on them but give them their space. And yes, sometimes the space gets so great that you may forget them, but they won't forget the food you put in their bowl and when they are ready to really eat spiritually, they will come find you.

Don't forget to keep some food in the bowl.

What's the POINT?

1. Who have you given up on?
2. How can you give space but keep pursuing an unbeliever?
3. Who came to Christ because you didn't give up on them?

CHAPTER 14

Tell Them the Good News

Tell them the Good News.
Jesus loves them and can change their lives forever.

"For God so loved the world that he gave his only Son, so that everyone who believes in him will not perish but have eternal life. 17 God did not send his Son into the world to *condemn* it, but to *save* it."

John 3:16–17

This is the Good News!

Jesus came to save people, not condemn them.

If Jesus isn't condemning the lost world, then why are we?

Oftentimes when I give this talk, I will ask the audience a question just as I want to ask you the question now.

What is your purpose in life? Do you know what God's purpose is for the church?

Let me ask it another way so you can think about what your calling and purpose is as the body of Christ.

Have you ever seen the movie, *Lord of the Rings*?

Frodo is the main character in the movie. He has been given a task, a calling, and a responsibility. What was Frodo's purpose in the *Lord of the Rings*?

I know.

He was to destroy the ring.

Was that his primary purpose?

No, his primary purpose was to *save* Middle-earth.

God gave each of us a positive redemptive purpose in life. God gave the church a positive redemptive purpose in life as well.

Unfortunately, the church today thinks its calling is to destroy the darkness and evil that permeates our society. It seems the church of America is on a political crusade to destroy evil. And yes, we do have to stand against evil just as Frodo did in the *Lord of the Rings*. We must fight against the darkness of this world. But it is NOT our primary calling and responsibility. Our primary calling and responsibility is to do what Christ came to do:

Jesus said in Luke 19:10,

> "And I, the Son of Man, have come to seek and *save* those like him (referring to Zacchaeus) who are lost."

Religion wants to destroy evil. Jesus wants to save the world. What do you want to be a part of?

I believe that the religion of Christianity is the biggest obstacle to people coming to Christ in our world today.

Jesus wants us to be about the business of seeking and asking him to save those who are lost. He wants us to stop cursing the darkness and start spreading the light. He wants us to stop focusing on what we are afraid of about this world and start asking Him to use us to bear upon our bodies the marks and sacrifice that is required to stand against the enemy and the evil forces of this world, so that people can experience through us not just the *right* ways to live but ultimately the love of Jesus Christ.

We are His servants created to do *good* works to bring glory to Him.

Has the enemy convinced you that you have a negative calling on your life? Are you convinced that you must stamp out sin in this world as your primary focus?

Do you realize it is not your primary job to restrain evil, but reveal the good news?

It is our job to love. It is our job to make love the supreme focus and approach to our sharing of the Good News of Jesus Christ with others.

1 Corinthians 13:1 says,

> If I could speak any language in heaven or on earth but didn't love others, I would only be making meaningless noise like a loud gong or a clanging cymbal. 2 If I had the gift of prophecy, and if I knew all the mysteries of the future and knew everything about everything, but didn't love others, what good would I be? And if I had the gift of faith so that I could speak to a mountain and make it move, without love I would be no good to anybody. 3 If I gave everything I have to the poor and even sacrificed my body, I could boast about it; but if I didn't love others, I would be of no value whatsoever.

The passage is pretty clear. Without love, the church is worthless.

I believe the church of America is becoming more and more worthless every day. Not because we don't have the potential or ability to be worthful, but because we would rather judge the world than love the world. We would rather share the Gospel with people instead of live the Gospel among people. We would rather tell people they are going to hell than feel the hell they are going through right now.

God is not okay with our judgmental spirits that seem to be prevalent in our churches today, similar to what the Pharisees were like when He came to this earth.

I live in a city full of Christians who believe that politics is going to save them.

I don't.

I firmly believe Christians should be involved in the political process and should work the political process to try and help their candidate(s) succeed. This gives us a voice as Americans who want this country to be influenced by the Judeo-Christian values that this country was founded on a longtime ago.

More power to all who choose to be a responsible citizen in the political process of our country.

However, politics void of relationship is death to the Gospel.

In a postmodern world we can't influence people if we are not in relationship with them, and more and more the church is becoming further removed from the society that it exists to reach. I am not talking about being relevant. I am talking about being real. I am talking about living, breathing, and rubbing shoulders among those who, in Jesus' day, they called "despicable and notorious sinners."

Do you know any notorious sinners? Would you or your church be called "a friend of sinners"?

Would you be proud to take a "sinner" to your church? Would they hear the Good News of Jesus Christ or just everything that is wrong with them and the rest of this world? I am not saying compromise the Bible. At our church we teach that homosexuality is "a" sin but it is not "the" sin. We teach what Jesus taught about the morals of his day that translate equally into our day.

I don't want to just share information with people without also being willing to hear and understand how that information affects them. I want to share my life with others through real relationship with Jesus and them.

A number of years ago, I got a call from the *Independent Newspaper*. It is known as our liberal left-wing newspaper here in Colorado Springs. Because of our involvement with community discussions in the past regarding world religions and homosexuality, they wanted to meet with us.

I met with John Weiss. I thought John was a reporter from the newspaper. About halfway through the conversation, I discovered that John was the founder of the *Independent*. I was surprised.

He told us that our church had a reputation in the city of being a church that wanted to help people talk across the aisle. He saw us as a moderate voice that wanted to bring healing to the brokenness of our city.

We were honored that the community surrounding us had told him these things about us. He said in one day no less than three times our name got mentioned to him.

The Bible says in 1 Timothy 3:7

Morever, he (the elder) must be well thought of by outsiders ...

Could this be said of your church and of your pastors and elders?

Colossians 4:5 says,

Walk in wisdom toward outsiders, making the best use of the time.

I want to ask the pastors who are reading this book a question: How long has it been since you have had an outsider in your office? How long has it been since you have had coffee with an outsider? How long has it been since you have done anything to reach out to the outside community outside of your preaching on Sunday morning?

Jesus came to seek and to save those who were lost. You are His shepherd.

Because of the "reputation" we had developed with outsiders, they came to us.

John asked us if we would be willing to host a community discussion.

Our church decided to partner with the leading liberal newspaper in our city. We agreed to bring the vice president of the NAE, Richard Cizik, to our church to talk about the issue of: "Would Jesus Go Green?"

We invited someone to give an opposing view to the NAE's view, but we could not secure a reputable presenter.

I wish I could say the evening went great, but it didn't. I felt like the evening was a bomb. John felt bad and so did I. Our church took a ton of heat not only from people outside the church, but also from people who attended our church. We had been a church long enough that "religion" was us now. It was sobering and humbling to realize that every church has its "religiosity," even the one you start.

I will save you the gory details, but suffice to say, I had a lot of egg to clean off my face and our church's face. I wanted us to host the community discussion so that we could build bridges of relationship into the unbelieving community and look for ways to find possible common ground. We did that, but the way it was presented was less than appealing or favorable.

The weeks that followed were tainted with criticism and verbal assault. We were accused of bringing Satan into the church. I was accused of doing Satan's work. How could that be? How could you be doing the Lord's work and be accused of doing Satan's work?

I seem to recall someone else who had to deal with this.

Luke 11:14 says,

One day Jesus cast a demon out of a man who couldn't speak, and the man's voice returned to him. The crowd was amazed, 15 but some said, "No wonder he can cast out demons. *He gets his power from Satan*, the prince of demons!"

Welcome to religion. If religious people don't like what you do or don't understand it, they will judge you by declaring you are doing the Lord's work in Satan's name and power.

This is a very painful accusation to have to carry, but rest assured if you try to reach the lost, the religious will criticize you. Maybe even crucify you. They did Jesus.

Satan is okay with us being religious, just don't get a real relationship with Jesus Christ.

We endured the criticism.

I asked our church to pray that John, the founder of the *Independent Newspaper*, would come and let me interview him about his spirituality. He is Jewish and does not believe in Jesus.

He was hesitant at first but through *relationship* he agreed.

I asked him these seven questions in front of our church. (I sent them to him prior so he could prepare to share.)

1. Tell us about you. Tell us your story and why you started the *Independent*.
2. Tell us why you do what you do? Why do you do humanitarian things? What motivates you?
3. What do you think about spirituality?
4. What do you think about Jesus?
5. What do you think about eternity?
6. What do you think about me trying to persuade you to have a REAL relationship with Jesus Christ?
7. Can I pray for you that you would have a REAL relationship with Jesus?

He agreed.

It was amazing. I was so nervous. He was nervous.

It may have very well been the best "church" service I have ever been to in my life.

It was a *redefining* moment in the life of our church.

It changed me.

It changed our church.

But most importantly, we pray, it would change John.

We prayed that the love of Jesus Christ would constrain him to be in real relationship with Him.

We have no power to cause this. We only have John 3:16–17. Jesus loves him and wants to save him. He wants to change him for good.

What about you? Has this book melted your hard heart toward the lost? Has this book refreshed you and rekindled your desire to love people into a real relationship with Jesus Christ?

The stories that I have shared with you in this book have changed my life and many other people's lives. But probably no story has changed me like the one I want to leave with you that will enable you to not only hear the Good News of the Gospel but see it and more importantly FEEL it.

Remember my ranting and ravings with God over not wanting to continue starting Vanguard? I wanted to run. I wanted to hide from my fear of failure. I wanted to lose myself in my selfish fear. I wanted to save face.

Just a few weeks after that experience of wanting to quit and come up with a justification for doing so, my wife and I went to Virginia Beach, Virginia, for Christmas with her family in 1996.

We went to First Baptist Norfolk. The senior pastor at the time was Bob Reccord. He was the man who had inspired us to remain Southern Baptist at the Southern Baptist Convention in New Orleans in June 1996.

He was in the process of transitioning out of the pastorate into the new role of president of the North American Mission Board for the SBC. Tosha's folks at the time were stationed in Virginia Beach, and this was the church they attended.

We ended up there for their annual Christmas Eve service.

The service was like many other Christmas Eve services I had been to. It was festive and Christmacy.

We sat on the back row.

A few minutes into the service, a guy came in wearing a nice navy blue suit and sat down beside me. He had a little girl with him. I assume it was his daughter. She looked to be about six if my memory serves me correctly.

As the service wore on, I drifted into what the preacher was saying and out like many do when I preach. It's just the way it is.

About halfway through the message, I started to notice this little girl seated on her daddy's knee to my left. She did not look so good. At the time my wife and I did not have kids (we have five now), and so I didn't pay a whole lot of attention to her and the symptoms she was displaying.

I did notice, though, as the service went on that she went from a chipper little girl to docile and leaning up against her dad as she sat on his lap. I also started to notice her skin color turning from a pinkish color to pale to eventually green color. Yes, *green*. I must confess though as a married man with no kids, I had no idea what was about to occur.

This was church of all places.

Without warning, this little blonde-haired beautiful little girl opened her mouth and like a geyser out came the most hideous stream of vomit.

That's right, vomit.

What was her dad to do?

He did what I have since done many times: he took his hands to her face and attempted to catch the vomit while carrying her out to get her to the bathroom. The vomit ran down his arms and on to his very nice navy blue suit.

It was gross.

What would you do?

I would go home.

I would burn the suit.

I would probably throw up, too.

I wish I could say I cared what he did. But I didn't.

I was not a dad and I didn't give it much thought.

I just thought, *Gross, I am glad I am not him.*

Since that day, I have been him many times and if you have kids, I am sure you have as well.

I drifted back into the service and tried to forget the horrific experience I had just had at "church." It was Christmas, for crying out loud. I don't need vomiting kids sitting next to me at church.

In a few minutes he came back.

Can you believe that?

He came back.

He sat down right next to me.

I tried not to let him know but I couldn't help but sniff a little to see if it was still on him.

I know.

I'm bad.

He sat that little girl on his knee and right back into the service they were.

What happened next has marked my life and literally changed me for eternity sake.

This was a God-ordained moment that I will *never* forget.

On this night I got the Good News. I got the Gospel. I got the "God so loved the world...." I got the love of Jesus deposited deeply in my heart.

The little girl motioned for her daddy to lean down so she could ask him a question.

He leaned down.

If there is one thing I have learned over the years it is this, "Kids don't know how to whisper."

She tried, but kids don't whisper, they just yell in a hushed tone.

I heard her say, "Daddy, did I get that yucky stuff on you?"

I could see her face and the fear, embarrassment, and potential shame on her face.

Her daddy's response changed me forever.

He looked back at her with a big smile and said, "Yeah, you got that yucky stuff on me, but that's okay because I love you."

She smiled the biggest smile a little girl could ever smile.

Her daddy loved her regardless of her yucky stuff. He loved her regardless of what her yucky stuff did to him and his nice suit.

He loved her.

Jesus came to this earth and allowed humanity to nail him to the cross of Calvary for our sins. And just like that dad, he allowed us to throw up our yucky stuff all over him in the midst of a religious world.

Can't you just see Jesus in your mind? Can't you just see him tilting his head back on the cross and saying with the greatest compassion,

Go ahead, world, and throw up on me.
Just get your yucky stuff all over me because I love you.

That is what Jesus did for you and me.

That is what Jesus wants us to do for this world.

He wants us as the church to stretch out our hands past our religious judgmental spirits around this world and say to it, "Go ahead, world, throw up all over us. Just get your yucky stuff all over us because we love you."

This is what the church has been called to be.

The Good News is not a "what" but a "who."

It is Jesus and we are to be as He was and is.

Jesus wants us to BE the good news to people.

He wants us to represent Him to them.

He wants us to love them into a REAL relationship with Him.

Can you smell it?

It's puke, my friend. It is the yucky stuff of this world.

It's what church smells like when we are "friends of sinners."

Are you ready to point people to Jesus Christ through loving them into a REAL relationship with Jesus Christ?

Grab a towel and your heart, it is about to get messy.

What's the POINT?

1. Do you know what the Good News is? If so, what?
2. Who do you need to share the Good News with?
3. How can you let them get their yucky stuff on you?

About the Author

Kelly grew up on a dairy farm in Kentucky. He is a graduate of Liberty University (BS 1993) and Dallas Theological Seminary (ThM 1996)

After completing seminary, Kelly and his wife, Tosha, became qualified as church planter apprentices with the Home Mission Board of the Southern Baptist Convention. They moved to Colorado Springs to start Vanguard Church of Colorado Springs in 1997. Vanguard quickly raised local media attention as well as national attention in media outlets such as *Time*, *The 700 Club*, *Christianity Today*, *The New York Times*, and *ABC World News Tonight*. It is now one of the largest SBC churches in the state of Colorado. They expanded to two campuses in Palmer Lake, CO, in 2015.

Kelly has now served as the senior pastor of Vanguard for twenty years. They have seen 3188 people follow Christ in believer's baptism and have partnered to help plant forty-two other churches through the Frontline Church Planting Center. The

SBC declared Vanguard in 2014 to be one of the top thirty SBC churches in its size range regarding conversion rate.

Along the way, Kelly has spoken for the Billy Graham Evangelical Association. He coauthored *real marriage: where fantasy meets reality* with his wife, Tosha, in 2008.

In addition to being the husband of Tosha and the senior pastor of Vanguard Church, Kelly is the proud father of five children: Anastasha 19, Christianna 17, Joshua 14, Annalarie 12, and Journey Grace 9. Their family runs a small beef farm in Colorado Springs and love it. Having grown up in Kentucky, Kelly loves Kentucky Wildcat Basketball.

Endnotes

i. http://www.huffingtonpost.com/shane-l-windmeyer/dan-cathy-chick-fil-a_b_2564379.html

.